MANCHESTER CITY IN EUROPE

MANCHESTER CITY IN EUROPE

'WE WILL TERRIFY EUROPE!'

ANDREW WALDON

FONTHILL

First published 2012

Fonthill Media Limited
www.fonthillmedia.com
office@fonthillmedia.com

Copyright © Andrew Waldon, 2012

The right of Andrew Waldon to be identified as the Author of this work has been asserted in accordance with the Copyrights, Designs and Patents Act 1988.

ISBN: 978-1-78155-077-9 (print)
ISBN: 978-1-78155-218-6 (e-book)

All rights reserved. No part of this book may be reprinted or reproduced or utilised in any form or by any electronic, mechanical or other means, now known or hereafter invented, including photocopying and recording, or in any information storage or retrieval system, without the permission in writing from the Publishers.

British Library Cataloguing in Publication Data.
A catalogue record for this book is available from the British Library.

Typeset in 11pt on 13.5pt Celeste.
Typesetting by Fonthill Media Limited
Printed and bound in England.

Connect with us
facebook.com/fonthillmedia   twitter.com/fonthillmedia

CONTENTS

1968-69 European Cup	9
1969-70 European Cup Winners' Cup	12
1970-71 European Cup Winners' Cup	32
Player Q&A	46
1970-71 Anglo Italian Cup	49
1972-73 UEFA Cup	52
Player Q&A	55
1976-77 UEFA Cup	56
1977-78 UEFA Cup	58
1978-79 UEFA Cup	61
Player Q&A	74
2003-04 UEFA Cup	79
2008-09 UEFA Cup	89
2010-11 Europa League	115
2011-12 Champions League/Europa League	142
2012-13 Champions League	159

ACKNOWLEDGEMENTS

This book has taken some time in coming to fruition, as the idea was first muted a number of years ago. So thanks to those that responded with their stories and photographs at the time and thanks to those ex-players who returned my Q&A.

Inevitably, newspapers have been consulted both nationally and locally and the power of the worldwide web has also greatly assisted. The photographs have come from the author's own collection as well as past issues of the Manchester City programme.

All statistics have been checked to the excellent *Manchester City: The Complete Record* by Gary James.

Finally I would like to thank Fonthill Media for giving me an opportunity to write about Manchester City again and to Bernadetta Cummings & Jessica Waldon for their support and to my son Daniel for his contributions; maybe this will inspire him to put his own literary talent to good use.

INTRODUCTION

Manchester City qualified for the European Cup following their League Championship success in 1967/68. Immediately after winning the title City manager Malcolm Allison said 'We'll terrify the cowards of Europe'. Inevitably, therefore, they lost their first ever European tie against the unfashionable Turkish champions, Fenerbahçe.

Since that date the clubs supporters have witnessed the highs and lows that European football can produce. Notable victories over the best teams in Europe, Gornik in the European Cup Winners' Cup in Vienna, remains clear in the memory as do those matches we would rather forget, Fenerbahçe in 1968, Borussia in 1978, right up to present date, where the club promised so much but left the supporters disillusioned.

This is an evocative collection covering 44 years (up to end of 2011–12) of how the media perceived the games, player's memories, supporters European trips, action shots, programme covers and assorted memorabilia. Illustrated here is the story of City through the triumph and disappointment of epic struggles against the best teams on the continent.

So as we head into the future we recall the past.

1968-69 EUROPEAN CUP

MANCHESTER CITY 0   FENERBAHÇE 0

European Cup
First Round – First Leg, Wednesday 18 September 1968
Maine Road, Manchester
Attendance 38,787

City Team: Mulhearn, Kennedy, Pardoe, Doyle, Heslop, Oakes, Lee, Bell, Summerbee, Young, Coleman

MANAGEMENT VIEW
We have played foreign teams on tours in friendly matches and at club level, tonight we began European competition in earnest. **(Joe Mercer)**

We will terrify Europe. **(Malcolm Allison)**

Malcolm is the sort of fellow you expect to make outrageous statements which take a lot of seriousness out of the grim business of professional football. He worries me a little but these statements are expected and accepted by just everyone in football. In fact they are regarded at times as a bit of a giggle. **(Joe Mercer)**

PLAYER VIEW
It was unfortunate that it was our first experience of Europe and it could not have been a bigger tournament. They kicked us up in the air; picked us up, shook our hands and we accepted it. **(Colin Bell)**

We all thought we were unbeatable and lost that edge. **(Mike Summerbee)**

For me the biggest disappointment was Fenerbahçe in the European Cup. It was Malcolm's fault really, because he never had them watched beforehand. He told us 'don't worry we will murder this lot'. We should have won the tie at Maine Road. We hit the bar about five times and it should have been 7-0 to us. In the end it was a goalless draw. **(Neil Young)**

PRESS VIEW
Feasted for so long on the talents of Bert Trautmann, Maine Road supporters last night had to take their hats off to another great foreign keeper the like of which probably has not been seen on the ground since Trautmann retired. Yavuz Simack an Under 23

international was chaired off the field and given a tremendous ovation after a superb display. (*Daily Telegraph*)

Manchester City must be hanging their heads in shame after a European Cup debut that saw them only able to draw, no score, at home to Turkish outsiders, Fenerbahçe. (*Daily Mirror*)

Manchester City the champions for whom nothing has gone right this season, fumbled and stumbled their way into Europe last night, in a galling goalless draw with Turkish rivals Fenerbahçe. (*Daily Mail*)

City fumble to goalless draw with Turks.

City trembled as the Turks broke out of defence from time to time to try to take back a lead for the return leg at Istanbul in a fortnight.

Even for the non-partisan spectators in the crowd it was sad to see the English champions so pathetically out of touch.

It was even more sickening to see thousands streaming out of the ground more than ten minutes before the end.

Manchester City's forwards frittered away at least five good scoring chances.

Star of the match was the Turk's brilliant 20-year old goalkeeper Simsek Yavuz.

FENERBAHÇE 2   MANCHESTER CITY 1

Goal Scorer: Coleman
European Cup
First Round – Second Leg, Wednesday 2 October 1968
Bayrampasa Stadyumu, Istanbul
Attendance: 45,000

City Team: Mulhearn, Connor, Pardoe, Doyle, Heslop, Oakes, Lee, Bell, Summerbee, Young, Coleman

PRE-MATCH ADVICE
City players must always remember to bring the ball back for a free kick. They would do well to throw flowers to the crowd before the match. Treat them with a cheerfulness and courtesy and things will be okay. Disobey this code of conduct and you could be in trouble. The crowd gets angry and so do the players. (**Malik Clin, ex-Fenerbahçe player**)

PLAYER VIEW
They really knocked the stuffing out of us. (**Alan Oakes**)

The score was about right. We made mistakes and we paid for them. I thought both their goals should never have happened. They were both from scrimmages but we have no excuse. There is a very hard lesson to be learned. You simply cannot make silly defensive mistakes in this type of competition and expect to get away with it.

I was injured for the game, but travelled with the team for the second leg. I remember getting up early on the match of the morning and drawing the curtains to see huge queues forming at the stadium in the alley below. This was hours before the game was due to start and it made me realise we were in for a tough afternoon.

The journey to the ground was somewhat unsettling too, as we passed armed guards and riot police along the way, and these were for the home fans. There was a great turnout from City fans as usual and we even took the lead through Tony Coleman but they were strong and came back to win 2-1. (**Tony Book**)

PRESS VIEW
Manchester City departed from their first European Cup competition to a patriotic din of claxon horns, fireworks and manifest Turkish delight. (***Daily Telegraph***)

A Turk who jetted in from Washington sent Manchester City out of the cup. The champions of England were the biggest casualties, beaten by Fenerbahçe.

Altinparmark Ogun recalled from Washington Whips scored the 77th minute winner and fans lit bonfires in the three-tier stadium. (***Daily Mirror***)

1969-70 EUROPEAN CUP WINNERS' CUP

ATHLETIC BILBAO 3   MANCHESTER CITY 3

Goal Scorers: Booth, Young, Echebaria (OG)
European Cup Winners' Cup
First Round – First Leg, Wednesday 17 September 1969
Estadio San Mamés, Bilbao
Attendance: 45,000

City Team:
Corrigan, Book, Pardoe, Doyle, Booth, Oakes, Summerbee, Bell, Lee, Young, Bowyer

PRESS VIEW

FA Cup holders Manchester City went across to Bilbao where they met Atleticos men who are now managed by former Wolves boss, Ronnie Allen. City were behind but they fought back to a more cheerful 3-3 final score and must be happy about the return to Manchester. (***Daily Express***)

Manchester City heckled and humiliated when they went out of the champions cup to Fenerbahçe last season discovered once more in Bilbao last night that Europe is a tough, tense and demanding battlefield. (***Daily Telegraph***)

Battling back from 3-1 down in Bilbao, Manchester City drew 3-3 to give the outstanding British performance on European soccer night. (***Daily Mail***)

Manchester City finally made it here tonight. From the unbelievably bad they eventually came good to achieve the psychological break through from which they can emerge as a European power. (***Daily Mirror***)

Magnificent City climb from brink of disaster

Manchester City fought back bravely from the brink of European humiliation here tonight.

After a nerve shattering start to their first Cup Winners Cup tie, they came through with an honourable draw to what may well now be a commanding position against Atletico Bilbao.

Two down after 11 minutes and run almost dizzy in defence; City reeled under blows that would have crushed the spirit of many sides.

But even after being 3-1 in arrears after 57 minutes they stubbornly refused to accept the defeat that 45,000 buoyant Basque supporters regarded as inevitable.

Dominating the later stages of the game, they drew level through a goal by Tommy Booth and one which Spanish captain Echeberia turned into his own net when under stern pressure from Colin Bell.

The full measure of City's resounding comeback is almost certain to be seen in the second leg at Maine Road, for away goals count double in this tournament if the scores finish up level.

MANAGEMENT VIEW

The lads are not satisfied. They were a bit niggled at the end because they thought they could have won, but wait until we play the second leg. We will play aggressively and really give Bilbao something to think about. **(Malcolm Allison)**

Last season we failed disappointingly in Istanbul and I am the first to hold up my hand and say we made a drastic mistake by not making any thorough preparations. Those same mistakes have not been made this time and I will tell you this, you will be proud to be British after the way you see them play tonight. **(Joe Mercer)**

I believe this can be the start of an exciting new era for Manchester City. An era where Maine Road is going to reverberate to the pulsating thrill of top European football. We have forgotten all about what happened in Turkey last season. The build-up has been different this time and the players are in a much different frame of mind. **(Joe Mercer)**

We are going to win 3-2. **(Malcolm Allison before the game)**

These boys have got the needle tonight because they did not win. Just wait until we get them back home. We will really give those Spaniards a roasting. **(Malcolm Allison after the game)**

Strangely enough, I did not feel too badly when Bilbao's second went in. Once Young scored I knew we would do well. Bilbao played far better than I expected, I was amazed when Arieta came off as I thought he was their best player. **(Joe Mercer)**

A wonderful result for us. We only started to play our normal game late in the first half. I knew we would come through once we could get our game going. **(Malcolm Allison)**

CAPTAIN'S VIEW

They really came at us early on with a lot of skill and of course got some goals. What surprised me was that when they were in front they seemed to relax a little and we were able to get back into the game. **(Tony Book)**

BILBAO VIEW

Iribar can be the best goalkeeper in the world. Tonight he was the worst. **(Ronnie Allen)**

SUPPORTER'S VIEW

I had just started working for British Rail and one of the perks of the job was free travel. So with City drawn to play Bilbao in Spain I could not think of a better and cheaper way to get there. Despite the threat of a French railway strike I made it to the Spanish border and eventually found the youth hostel where I was to be staying only to be confronted by the owner, who had bought the hostel and it was now his private home, so a hasty retreat was made.

A combination of hitchhiking and the train brought me to a boarding house in Bilbao, so with somewhere to rest my head I only had one minor problem left to sort out. I had no tickets for the game, only a letter from City saying I could get tickets at the ground before the match. I wandered down town to The San Mamés stadium and interrupted a press conference. To be told that I needed to go to the City team hotel on the other side of town.

Well with three tickets in hand after trekking up the hill to the team hotel, I met three fellow British Rail workers, who had arrived on the day of the match without tickets, so an hour before the match, we were wandering around trying to find someone to get tickets off. I was brandishing my letter on Manchester City headed paper, when a Spanish official directed me down a tunnel under the stand, he opened a door for me and I was in the City dressing room, because I was wearing my City shirt and had the letter in my hand they thought I was one of the City players lost in the crowd. Malcolm Allison did not fall for it though and with half a dozen comps in hand I beat a hasty retreat.

MANCHESTER CITY 3   ATHLETIC BILBAO 0

Goal Scorers: Bowyer, Bell, Oakes
European Cup Winners' Cup
First Round – Second Leg, Wednesday 1 October 1969
Maine Road, Manchester
Attendance: 49,665

City Team:
Corrigan, Book, Pardoe, Doyle, Booth, Oakes, Summerbee, Bell, Lee, Young, Bowyer

MANAGEMENT VIEW

Bilbao are a predictable side and we thought we would be able to find a way through the middle, but I admit I was getting worried when we went so long without scoring and when young Bowyer hit the bar I began to think it was going to be one of those nights, but that goal by Alan Oakes settled it. **(Joe Mercer)**

PLAYER VIEW

I hit it and it happened to go in, at a time when I was beginning to think we would never score. **(Alan Oakes)**

Joe Mercer and Malcolm had told us to go forward as Bilbao retreated and have a go. I remember I ran with the ball and shot it in. It was one of my greatest moments. **(Alan Oakes)**

The following comments were made after an incident had taken place in the tunnel as the players left the pitch at half time, when eye witnesses reported an alleged scuffle between Mike Doyle and Bilbao player Jose Ramon Betzuen.
I do not know what all the fuss is about. There was a bit of bother just before half time, but nothing serious. **(Mike Doyle)**

BILBAO VIEW

I had to take him off, he could hardly breathe, after that, we were finished. **(Ronnie Allen, Bilbao Manager)**

PRESS VIEW
Magnificent City blast the Europe nightmare.

Exciting Manchester City banished a bad dream last night when they blasted their way through to the second round of the Cup Winners Cup with a non-stop onslaught against defiant Atletico Bilbao.

The haunting memory of last season's dismal failure against Turkish champions Fenerbahçe nagged the mind of anxious supporters in the big crowd at Maine Road as frustration mounted for 59 frantic minutes.

But then came the long awaited break through that was accompanied by thunderous roars of relief.

Burly Alan Oakes, the longest serving player on City's staff, was the man who did what his forwards had so long failed to do. He stole the ball from the

Spanish side's 17 year old substitute, Ortuondo, strode forward a few paces and smacked it into the roof of the net from 25 yards.

A stubborn fight by a brave and besieged Spanish defence had ended. For Manchester City the rest was easy. Goals by Colin Bell and teenager Ian Bowyer confirmed their complete supremacy and established them as strong favourites for this European trophy.

LIERSE SK 0   MANCHESTER CITY 3

Goal Scorers: Lee (2), Bell
European Cup Winners' Cup
Second Round – First Leg, Wednesday 12 November 1969
Lierse Sportkring
Attendance: 18,000

City Team: Corrigan, Book, Pardoe, Doyle (Heslop), Booth, Oakes, Summerbee, Bell, Lee, Young, Bowyer

MANAGEMENT VIEW

This was a pleasing result for us and one I thought was right in every way. Lierse gave us a good fight and they played better than I thought possible. **(Joe Mercer)**

We played extremely well in our third European test and we were altogether too strong and professional for the Belgians. I thought Tommy Booth had a splendid match and was also pleased to see Joe Corrigan make a couple of fine saves near the end. **(Malcolm Allison)**

Lee and Bell in commanding form for City

Manchester City's cup-conscious footballers last night moved confidently and commandingly towards a place in the quarter finals of the European Cup Winners Cup in the small Belgian market town of Lier. They won a handsome first leg victory against Lierse SK in this second round tie with three well taken goals before half time.

Two came from Francis Lee and the third came from Colin Bell to make the Maine Road return a formality, and the skilful English forwards played dominant roles in a win that was emphatic and thoroughly deserved.

City took a firm grip on the proceedings in the seventh minute. Lee got in a smart overhead flick when Bell nodded on a corner by Summerbee and although Englen got his hand to the ball he could not keep it out of the net.

Lee and Bell exposed the shortcomings of Bogaerts and Michielsen time and time again and Lee who roved enterprisingly on the wings then accepted a shrewd pass from Young to cut in a drive a firm left-footed shot off an upright.

The third goal arrived in the 44th minute. Summerbee put Lee clear on the right and he went to the goal line before putting over a cross which left Bell with a simple opening six yards out.

SUPPORTER'S VIEW

One year on from the Fener-debacle, City had set out once again in their bid to conquer Europe. This time it was in the Cup Winners' Cup and we were drawn to play SK Lierse from Belgium. Being young, free and single, me and my pal Barry Batkin decided we were going to have a slice of this 'ere European scene. Not missing a domestic game, home or away for three years, we saw Lierse as the ideal adventure into Europe – not too distant but far enough to be interesting for two lads who previously had ventured only as far as the Dell! Unfortunately being young, free and single also included being skint. Not deterred by mere financial restrictions, we set about organising ourselves.

First time off work. Not too difficult for Barry as he had a reasonably enlightened employer and had holidays due anyway. Not so myself, I was told by then boss that if I insisted in taking time off to watch a bunch of 'nancies' running around kicking a bag of wind, then I should not bother to come back. I suppose that was only to be expected from an exiled Kiwi whose only previous experience of life was running the post office on the Cook Islands in the Pacific. He just could not grasp the significance of it all. For two long suffering City fans (some things don't change) who were suddenly beginning to enjoy football utopia, this seemed a million miles from the day we played Swindon in front of 8,015 or was it 80,015 as every City fan I know and ever known, claims to have been there. Anyway, I convinced myself that I could always get another job, they were ten a penny (some things do change) and got on with the task. Next step a letter to City re tickets and 'er. Excuse me, just where abouts is Lierse'. The reply was encouraging, tickets enclosed and directions – 'a few miles from Antwerp'. Where's Antwerp? The tickets cost 1.92*d* each (Yes City's sortie into Europe was pre-decimalisation, but the farthing had been dispensed with) and if my mathematics are correct that's about £1.46. To put that into perspective my first season ticket standing on the Kippax cost me £8.

We certainly could not afford to travel with the official supporter's party and other modes of transport were not practical, we reckoned it would be asking too much of my Honda 50 moped, to take both of us fully loaded, there and back. So we only had one option, being experienced hitchhikers, well we had done it before, usually when we missed the last bus from town on a Saturday night, we settled for that. How long would it take us? A straw poll of our friends indicated anything between 8 hours and 8 weeks. We decided to settle for a Sunday morning start and hope for the best.

Off we set, complete with compulsory hangover on a miserable, November Sunday morning. First major decision was North or South i.e. towards Maine Road or away? We tossed a coin and it turned out we were lucky. On the roundabout at Lymm we got our first lift. We just could not believe our luck, the guy was going all the way down to Essex, and he confirmed it was on the way to Belgium. So mid-afternoon we were dropped off somewhere off the A1. Not much progress was made for the rest of the day and in fact we ended up taking B&B in a very nice bus shelter (complete with glass) in Brentwood. It was freezing, but we did manage to get some sleep until about 3 a.m., when two very nice, friendly policemen wanted to welcome us to their beat. I saw them coming so pretended to be in a deep sleep. I judged that we would have a better chance, on a sympathy basis if a comatose Barry handled this one. Barry's response led to a grilling along the lines of a Spanish inquisition. We were not however helped by the fact that Barry chose this moment to forget his home address, so I stepped in with my silver tongue and explained to the two officers, the significance of the sky blue and white scarves and union jacks draped over us, that Colin Bell was next to god and Francis Lee was ten times better than anything Europe could produce. Convinced, I think, that we were not escapees from a nearby detention centre, but perhaps just a little misguided, they told us to 'push off and don't come back'.

So off we set again, next lift, and at about 6 a.m. was from a man delivering eggs. The egg man said he could take us on the way to where we could catch the ferry, but he had to make some deliveries on the way. About 8 hours and 10 dozen broken eggs later, we got out to find we had only progressed 2 miles further on.

We eventually made it to the docks only to find that the next ferry to Ostend would be in about 8 hours. Not to worry, we found a quiet hospitable watering hole and indulged in several half's and numerous games of bar billiards. A rather uneventful crossing, apart from Barry shouting for Hughie mid channel. But at least he did remember to put his teeth in his pocket this time, but that's another story. We arrived in Ostend early Tuesday and 'jumped' a train to Antwerp and arrived in Lierse in the afternoon, 24 hours before the kick-off.

After making our way to the ground, we decided to have a look at their social club and compare it with ours. It was not much. The beer, our introduction to proper lager was pleasant but the oncoming hunger was a cause for concern mainly for Piggy (sorry Barry), but he survived on litres of lager with those awful sickly foreign chocolate bars as chasers. The locals were a friendly bunch, for foreigners and before long the beer was flowing and on the house. We communicated in sign language, have you ever tried doing a Malcolm Allison impersonation after 10 pints? Fortunately their knowledge of the English game was excellent and the only disagreement concerned the other lot from Old Trafford, but we soon convinced them they were just a bunch of over hyped chancers who did not even belong to Manchester.

We stayed overnight in the club. Well what I mean is we woke up there. Morning of the match we took a walk around the village and renewed acquaintances with some of our previous night's drinking partners. We also met the local butcher who I think turned out to be the goalkeeper.

A hour or so before kick-off we went to the ground. Through the gates, flashing our tickets, which we were told were for the best seats. We were directed to a row of kitchen chairs set back a few yards off the touchline. It was certainly a good view; we had a lot to sing about as the boys romped home 3-0 on the night. We celebrated and somehow we got back home on the Friday, although I must admit I cannot for the life of me remember anything about the return journey.

I went to work as normal on the Monday morning and the Kiwi congratulated me and promptly docked me a week's wages, but at least I kept my job. **(Paul Priest)**

MANCHESTER CITY 5   LIERSE SK 0

Goal Scorers: Bell (2), Lee (2), Summerbee
European Cup Winners' Cup
Second Round – Second Leg, Wednesday 26 November 1969
Maine Road, Manchester
Attendance: 26,486

City Team: Mulhearn, Book, Pardoe, Doyle, Booth, Oakes (Towers), Summerbee, Bell, Lee, Jeffries, Bowyer

MANAGEMENT VIEW

We had one or two dicey moments in the early part of the game, when they could have scored twice, at least. If my forwards had those chances I would have expected them to score. The greasy pitch acted a bit as a leveller but in the end it went the way I expected. **(Joe Mercer)**

PLAYER VIEW

This performance by Lierse was one of the most sporting I have ever seen. It is an example to all European football. Trailing as they were before tonight, they knew they had little chance, we could have run a real risk of injury if they had got stuck in hard, but they played fair and they played well. We all felt like going in their dressing room at the end and thanking them. **(Francis Lee)**

LIERSE SK VIEW

Manchester City will go onto win this cup. We played better than we did on our own ground but the difference in class was too much. They are professionals, we are like amateurs. I was very pleased with the way we played. The score could have been 5-

3 because we missed some very good chances in the first half. I am glad we came up against Manchester City because this was a very good lesson for us. If I could I would come across to England to see them every month. **(Staf Van Den Berg, Lierse manager)**

City blast 8-0 message

Manchester City took one more stride towards the £30,000 jackpot for winning the European Cup Winners Cup as they disposed of Lierse at Maine Road last night.

It was the expected canter but not before City survived a terrific start. No less than three attempts at goal a split second of chaos in the City goalmouth failed to produce the stimulus the part timers needed. Goalkeeper Ken Mulhearn parried the first shot, the second was stopped on the line and the third scorched past an upright.

Andre De Nul also created havoc before City who had difficulty in keeping their balance on a greasy top surface-ended the Belgians faint hopes of survival with a goal from Mike Summerbee.

Three minutes after the interval the Belgians were finished. The defence failed to clear a free kick by Mike Doyle and a header by Ian Bowyer was followed up by Francis Lee.

City moved halfway towards the six goal target they had set themselves in the 55th minute when Bowyer glanced a centre by Alan Oakes across the goal and Lee headed the ball just inside an upright. These goals were part of 15 minutes of sheer terror for the Belgian side.

They were eventually sunk by two more goals from the scintillating Colin Bell, the first a header the next a fierce shot as City toyed with their rivals.

ACADEMICA COIMBRA 0   MANCHESTER CITY 0

European Cup Winners' Cup
Third Round – First Leg, Wednesday 4 March 1970
Municipal Stadium
Attendance: 8,000 to 15,000

City Team:
Corrigan, Book (Heslop), Mann, Doyle, Booth, Oakes, Pardoe, Bell, Summerbee, Lee, Young

MANAGEMENT VIEW

Perhaps both teams were a bit frightened of each other, but it is still a very pleasing result for us. I know it was not a classic but we got what we wanted. **(Joe Mercer)**

Book may miss final

Tony Book, the captain whose inspiration could mean so much to Manchester City in Saturdays Wembley League Cup Final, limped out of the Cup-winners' cup here last night with a painful ankle injury.

Joe Mercer said "Tony caught his studs on the laces of a Coimbra player and this caused him to fall awkwardly".

City, who had hoped to boost their morale for Wembley, sagged instead into a pre final trough of depression with a listless display. In a goalless first half, plodding City played well below the standard that will be needed for Wembley. The quarter final against the Portuguese became a craftless and colourless bore that even the fiercely partisan home supporters found little to raise their enthusiasm.

The frustration of both teams began to show after the interval when tempers became frayed and in the 54th minute City trainer Ewing was ordered to leave the touchline box for coaching his side. The former City centre half appeared to refuse at first to leave and then the referee and one of his linesmen pushed him away and he had to go.

We played much better in the second half and from our point of view it was a good result. (**Malcolm Allison**)

Ten minutes into the second half City trainer Dave Ewing was dismissed from his seat on the bench.

The City trainer was sent off for what I would call ungentle manly conduct. He was doing too much shouting and I will not allow this, but the incident is finished and forgotten. (**Robert Schaut, Belgian referee**)

It was very unfortunate. I always shouted as a player. I always shout now. The players claim that the only man who can understand my accent is Arthur Mann, but I have never been in this sort of trouble before and certainly never sent off. Apparently Belgian referees don't allow trainers and coaches to do any sort of shouting from the touchline, so that was that. (**Dave Ewing**)

PLAYER VIEW

We did not know a great deal about Academica but we soon found out they were a very dirty side. Every one of them would run past you and spit at you in an attempt to get you riled. (**Neil Young**)

MANCHESTER CITY 1   ACADEMICA COIMBRA 0

Goal Scorer: Towers
European Cup Winners' Cup
Third Round – Second Leg, Wednesday 18 March 1970
Maine Road, Manchester
Attendance: 36,338

City Team:
Corrigan, Book, Mann, Booth, Heslop (Towers), Oakes, Doyle, Bell (Glennon), Lee, Young, Pardoe

PRESS VIEW

The first goal, young Tony Towers, has scored in senior football put Manchester City into the semi-finals of the European Cup Winners' Cup after a desperate rugged extra time battle against the Portuguese student side, Academica Coimbra. (*Daily Telegraph*)

Tony Towers an 18 year old substitute saved Manchester City the agony of a trial by a play off in Amsterdam to finish this Cup Winners' Cup clash. He scored in the final seconds of extra time to put City in the last four and break a goalless deadlock. (*Daily Mirror*)

Substitute Tony Towers scored in the last minute of extra time to steer Manchester City through to the semi-final of the European Cup Winners' Cup. He climaxed a frustrating two hours of football by City, who despite having all the play were thrown out of their stride by the rough and sometimes crude tackling Portuguese students. (*Daily Mail*)

Cool sub takes the heat off City

Manchester City's flair for the big occasion almost failed them last night when they were forced into extra time by a team of £50 a month part timers from Portugal. Their second leg of the Cup-Winners' Cup quarter final against Academica Coimbra had stuttered along untidily to the point at which there was only one minute to go to a play off in Amsterdam.

Never could there have been a moment of greater need for a goal scoring hero to emerge, and when it did, City's man of destiny turned out to be Tony Towers the 17-year old half back who had won his first place in his first European role as a substitute when George Heslop had to drop out at half time because of a gashed knee. The last few seconds were ticking away when Towers let fly and City could breathe again.

CHAIRMAN COMMENT

We can't offer Academica anything of the scenic quality of Portugal, nor can we even guarantee the weather, but I hope we can offer the Players, Directors and Supporters of the club the same sort of friendly welcome they gave us. Whatever the result I hope they will be able to look back at Maine Road, Manchester and the people they meet here on the terraces and behind the scenes with affection and admiration. (**Albert Alexander, Club Chairman**)

COIMBRA VIEW ON SHIRT ISSUE

The referee said he would look a clown if he appeared in red or blue, but he had to change to a white strip. We were serious when we said we would not play if we could not turn out in Black. It is a centuries old tradition and very important for Coimbra. (**Joao Altido, a Coimbra & Portuguese FA representative**)

FC SCHALKE 04 1   MANCHESTER CITY 0

European Cup Winners' Cup
Semi Final – First Leg, Wednesday 1 April 1970.
Gluckauf Stadium
Attendance: 38,000

City Team: Corrigan, Book, Pardoe, Doyle, Jeffries, Oakes, Booth, Bell, Lee, Young, Summerbee

PRESS VIEW

A majestic, inspiring and unfortunate Manchester City tasted European Cup Winners' Cup defeat for the first time in this semi-final. A stylish City show suddenly turned sour on them on 78 minutes when German right winger Libuda swept Schalke into the lead. (*Daily Mirror*)

Reinhard Libuda, whose goal for Dortmund beat Liverpool in the final of the same competition four years ago, shot from a solo run to put Joe Mercers men a goal down in the first leg of this semi-final. (*Daily Mail*)

Manchester City who obviously prefer the more tangible rewards of cup fighting to normal first division business, produced one of their best displays in European competition but still lost a demanding first leg semi-final through a 78th minute goal from Libuda. The concession of that important late goal was a bitter blow to City. (*Daily Telegraph*)

MANAGEMENT VIEW

We are going to complain against the booking Summerbee got for kicking the ball into the crowd. It was a misunderstanding Mike did not hear the refs whistle. There was no question of it being a gesture of dissent. It was a tough game, a fair game but I think we will be there at the end. **(Joe Mercer)**

We can win the semi-final at Maine Road, if we attack but we need the right atmosphere. All of us want our supporters to roll up and back our efforts. **(Malcolm Allison)**

I was disappointed with the result but very satisfied with the performance. Libuda scored a good goal, but it was hard on us after we had done so much. The tie is far from over yet. We can do it at home. **(Joe Mercer)**

SUPPORTER'S TALE

Thanks to a friend of mine, who had a mate who lived in Dusseldorf, who was going to be the translator for the English press for the game, any worries about finding somewhere to stay were put at ease.

The actual journey to Germany can best be described as non-descript, ferry and then a train to Dusseldorf. So after a good night sleep following our arrival, we were on the coach to pick up the English press for the short trip to the ground in Gelsenkirchen. We followed the players' coach to the ground which incidentally was enclosed by gates and a fence. The gateman clearly had instructions to only allow one coach in, so the team get in and the press are locked out. Eventually an apologetic club official comes to our rescue, so in goes the coach and two dozen City fans without tickets

MANCHESTER CITY 5   FC SCHALKE 04 1

Goal Scorers: Young (2), Bell, Lee, Doyle
European Cup Winners' Cup
Semi Final – Second Leg, Wednesday 15 April 1970
Maine Road, Manchester
Attendance: 46,361

City Team: Corrigan, Book, Pardoe, Doyle (Heslop), Booth, Oakes, Towers, Bell, Lee, Young, Summerbee (Carrodus)

PRESS VIEW

Neil Young dropped in January, re-appeared as the hero of Manchester City at Maine Road when he scored two great goals. (*Daily Mirror*)

Manchester City a club which romps from one cup success to another in bewildering fashion, strode magnificently into the European Cup Winners' Cup Final with a handsome, commanding victory. (*Daily Telegraph*)

Manchester City went imperiously into the European Cup Winners' Cup Final, shattering Schalke 5-2 on aggregate. (*Daily Mail*)

Manchester City the big game hunters of soccer, shook of their dismal league form last night and galloped into the final. Schalke were not beaten, they were crushed by a spectacular display of forward power. (*Daily Express*)

City's five goal waltz to Vienna

Manchester City waltzed in quick time to Vienna last night with a scintillating 5-1 win in the second league of their European Cup-winner's Cup against Schalke 04.

So utterly overwhelming was their superiority and so merciless were their marksmen that the result was never, even for the briefest moment, in doubt.

City the team who reserve their champagne sparkle for the big occasions soared to heights greater than ever before to run their West German foes into a state of almost pitiable dismay and disarray.

The Germans did get a face saving goal in injury time when keeper Joe Corrigan dived and turned a shot to the feet of the famous but inconspicuous Libuda who had only to tap it into the net. But it had been a heroic effort even for Corrigan to turn out. Earlier in the day his nose had been broken in a collision with reserve keeper Ken Mulhearn during a game of head tennis.

City's rousing, runaway success was a triumph of tremendous team work and non-stop running as well as tactics for which manager Joe Mercer and his assistant Malcolm Allison deserved great credit.

MANAGEMENT VIEW

Don't be impatient, take this game in your stride and above all go out and play as a team. (**Malcolm Allison**)

Schalke are a powerful, tight marking side with an experienced sweeper on Fichtel and I do not expect them to falter under heavy pressure. We have got to run at them, turn them and continually worry them if we are to create the gaps and get the two goals we need. (**Joe Mercer**)

A great performance, it was really thrilling to watch. They played as Malcolm and I wanted them to, full of flair, drive and imagination and tore Schalke apart. We can talk tactics all week but the players have to go out and do the job. They did so admirably. (**Joe Mercer**)

PLAYER VIEW

In January I thought I would have little chance of getting back into the first team. I seemed to have lost all my confidence, but once I scored that first goal, the whole game seemed an exciting challenge. **(Neil Young)**

We were 1-0 down from the first leg and I scored the goal that levelled the scores. They were strong opponents and about half of their team were regulars for the West German side. **(Mike Doyle)**

SCHALKE VIEW

I feel City will win the cup. If they show this effort in the final. We were depressed when we lost those early goals and obviously I am disappointed with our performance. City were lucky in that three shots gave them three goals. That is not normal for them, but they were beautiful goals. **(Rudi Gutendorf, Schalke coach)**

GORNIK ZABRZE 1   MANCHESTER CITY 2

Goal Scorers: Lee (P), Young
European Cup Winners' Cup
The Final, Wednesday 29 April 1970
Prater Stadium, Vienna, Austria
Attendance: 7,968 to 12,000

City Team: Corrigan, Book, Pardoe, Doyle (Bowyer), Booth, Oakes, Heslop, Bell, Lee, Young, Towers,

PLAYER & MANAGEMENT VIEW

The last time we played in Europe, we failed miserably going out to Fenerbahçe. We were overconfident but we have not made that mistake this season and we can win this cup. **(Joe Mercer before the game)**

My team had orders to attack whenever there was a chance. It paid off; defences must be driven into the ground with the utmost individual determination when chances come. That's why I like to see brave wingers stretch defences until they suddenly snap in the middle. With this victory the lads really won by four or five goals. **(Joe Mercer after the game)**

Our supporters did us proud in Vienna and we are proud of them. Perhaps the lads did not play as well as they can but we were supremely confident from the word go. Now it seems to be coming a bit of a habit picking up all these cups. **(Joe Corrigan)**

I was never in any real doubt about the result. We were the better equipped side all round and Gornik were a disappointing team. **(Glyn Pardoe)**

We won because we have so much team spirit. Everyone works for one and other. **(Mike Doyle)**

Gornik, so were told are supposed to have a useful attack, but it did not impress me, perhaps we did not play as well as we can but quite honestly we were the better side. **(Tommy Booth)**

When our second goal (that penalty) went in I knew we were home, but we had to play a bit defensively in the second half, something that is a bit foreign to our nature, however I was proud of the way the boys rallied when the going became tough. **(Tony Book)**

No doubt about it, we were the better team all round. We were well on top until Mike Doyle was injured halfway through the first half and but for that we could have goals won by four or five goals. **(Alan Oakes)**

We did not do as well as we did in the League Cup Final but I can tell you this. The players were determined to do well and we all went out there with a will to win. The aim was to keep check of Lubanski and I think we did that job well enough. **(George Heslop)**

I don't think we played well at all. In fact at times we were only moderate, but we did enough to win and that is the important fact. We got the initiative from the start and never let go from then on. **(Colin Bell)**

We won this game in the first half hour. We took our chances and clinched it in that vital spell. They were apprehensive about attacking us and that was the point on which the game hinged and you can say I was a bit pleased when that goal of mine went in. **(Neil Young)**

I thought Ian Bowyer did a tremendous amount of chasing and all credit must go to him for the way he worked when coming on as a substitute. From my own point of view, the game I played was not my normal role, but I thought they shot their bolt in the second half. **(Tony Towers)**

The first goal was the real incentive. The second a killer, so far as Gornik were concerned. We never looked like losing from that point. They scored a lucky goal to get back into the game but frankly it was the only shot on target they really had in 90 minutes and despite the atrocious conditions of the second half, we all worked extremely hard. **(Francis Lee)**

I never at any time thought there was any danger of losing. **(Mike Summerbee)**

We made a great start and built from there. We won the game in midfield in the first half and thought we might have lost it a bit after half time. I thought the lads worked so hard for each other that we were never in any real danger. **(Ian Bowyer)**

Naturally the goals won it for us, but the overriding factor was that we had the moral courage to have a go at them. If Mike Doyle had not had to come off we would have won by a distance. **(Joe Mercer)**

I did not think they ever looked like scoring and the goal they did get was a fluky affair. I thought George Heslop had a great game. **(Malcolm Allison)**

There were doubts over as to how many City fans would go to the final.
'We just do not know how many are going. Fourteen planes, dozens of cars and coaches and goodness knows how many are travelling by rail and sea or making the trip.' **(Walter Griffiths, City Secretary)**

SUPPORTERS' TALES

Me and my mate Barry have a claim to fame, which came about from attending the final in Vienna. We had saved enough money to take a package trip, 30 guineas it cost for three nights in Vienna.

On a dreadful night in the open air, Prater Stadium, soaked inside as well as out, we spotted the dynamic duo, Joe and Mal, sat not too far away. We clambered across railings, barbed wire and approached where they were sat, guarded by gun bearing 'Gestapo'. Literally at gunpoint we begged them to let us through. With encouragement from Joe we were allowed through and took up position next to our heroes. Gob smacked was not invented then but we were and truly, so much so, that the alcohol induced bravado that prompted us to take such a risk, left us almost immediately and neither of us could pluck up the courage to talk to either of them. We could hardly believe it, Joe and Mal, sat there drenched to the skin, with towels on their heads, next to us.

One half of the magical partnership never said a word and the other did not shut up, bellowing across the vast empty stadium, his every instruction lost in the driving rain. You would be forgiven for assuming it was Mal doing the shouting. I was certainly surprised to watch him sit there, motionless, quietly confident that he had done his work and it was now down to the boys. On the other hand Joe was a nervous wreck, fidgeting, gibbering, and cursing. Poor Colin Bell came in for some stick. 'Baron' he kept shouting, 'do this, do that, get back, get forward', but ultimately, smiling, that wonderful smile, from ear to ear, like a Cheshire cat, it was magic, absolute magic.

It was a memory to cherish, witnessing at close quarters the greatest managerial team, enjoying arguably their finest hour with their team, the greatest this country has ever produced and the likes of which we will sadly never be seen again. **(Paul Priest)**

The trip to Vienna to watch the 1970 Cup Winners' Cup Final between City and Gornik was a dream come true to all City fans. City our team in a major European Cup Final!

The trip itself was on an organised basis by the club and for 30 Guineas (yes Guineas), we were flown to Vienna on the day of the game from Manchester Airport; also included in the price was a match ticket, overnight accommodation, plus a coach from the hotel to the stadium,

What seems very odd years later is the dress code used by lots of fans, the fact being that most supporters travelled in suits or jackets and trousers, a quite formal way to dress for a football match, but at the time it seemed the norm. I had a new light grey suit, with only a scarf, which I still possess and a rosette to show my support, no face painting in 1970. The game itself was a rather strange affair. The Prater Stadium was a very large open ground with absolutely no cover whatsoever. About 5,000 City fans had made the journey but Gornik had only two to three hundred supporters who had travelled from behind the Iron Curtain in coaches, which looked like they had been built in the 1930s. The reason given for the poor attendance was that the game was televised throughout Europe, that is except in England, where the FA Cup replay between Chelsea and Leeds United was taking place somewhere near Manchester in Stretford. To this day City is the only English team to have played a major European Cup Final and not had it televised live in England.

The match itself started, after my struggle to get my programme, which was free. The evening was very warm and humid, ideal for football. City were very quickly into their stride and after only 12 minutes took the lead through Neil Young (Nelly). It was not longer after this that the first signs of rain began to show, gradually the rain got harder and harder, but minutes before then interval, City increased their lead from the penalty spot after Neil Young had been brought down, Lee 1 pen converted and it was 2-0 at half time. We were jubilant it was in the bag, surely, but then again this was Manchester City. The rain was now incessant with not one ounce of cover or shelter to be had. Gornik did manage to pull a goal back late in the game through Ozlizlo, but by now our main concern was the rain not Gornik, the pitch had become a quagmire and we were getting drenched.

The final whistle eventually arrived, the relief and jubilation in equal measures was immense but even more remarkable was that the downpour suddenly ceased as if to salute Manchester City the winners of the 1970 Cup Winners' Cup. Eventually we left the ground, both hoarse and delirious looking like a bunch of drowned rats, but who cared we had triumphed in Europe. City were on the map big style.

As for my new light Grey suit, it was ruined, but that was a small price to pay for the pleasure and joy of watching City win in Europe. **(Roland Griffin, RIP)**

Twelve of us mustered in the Beehive pub in Whitefield on the Friday prior to the 1970 European Cup Winners' Cup final in Vienna, to load up a 12-seater mini bus we had conned off somebody's dad. Being totally skint at the time we took all our own provisions, which we packed onto the roof rack. Our first moment of excitement came when I turned sharp right at the traffic lights at Heaton Park. The entire contents of the roof rack shifted violently to one side almost pulling the wreck of a mini bus over into the main road. After quickly re-arranging all our tins of beans, etc., under the seats we continued onto our next near death experience. Half way down the M6 some of the luggage left on top of the mini bus decided to throw itself across a couple of lanes of the motorway causing something less than merriment amongst fellow road users.

We eventually arrived at Dover in pouring rain sometime during Saturday, to be told our scheduled hovercraft would be delayed due to sea's conditions. Allowed to board after some delay, with the firm instructions to remain seated throughout the voyage or risk serious injury. On arriving at Calais, the first thing that met my eyes was a gun-toting gendarme; I had never seen a gun before. We were not too long on our journey into France when we got our mandatory puncture just as it was turning dark. I got totally annoyed at the number of French drivers who blasted their horns at us as I struggled to fit the spare, nobody told me I was supposed to display a triangle in the event of a breakdown.

My mate Patsy took over the driving to allow me a deserved kip as I had done most of the driving up until this point. I was awoken from my deep slumber somewhere in the French country side by a huge bump and the sight of the recently changed wheel overtaking us. All four studs had sheared leaving us completely stuck in the middle of nowhere on a Saturday night, Sunday morning. Eventually Monday came and we were able to find a mechanic in some rural outback that welded the wheel studs back on for us for almost nothing. Overwhelmed with gratitude we showered him with duty free cigs and a City scarf.

The German border guards welcomed us with open arms; they also opened every item of luggage and even subjected some of us to a strip search. Whilst we all made it to Vienna the van never did, we had no choice but to leave the wreck at a home for chronically sick motors somewhere near Munich to undergo lifesaving surgery.

I eventually reached Vienna in a rainstorm after hitchhiking and spending the night in an Austrian barn trying to get some sleep. Finding the Prater stadium was not much fun as most of the locals did not know where it was or that a major football final was being played in their City. The only thing worth remembering about the game was that we won 2-1 and all I wanted was a good night's sleep. Somehow all of us managed to meet up and found a cheap hotel; I say hotel but it was more a hostel used by the down and outs of Vienna and the ladies of the night.

Only ten of us managed to recover the mini bus from its sick bed, the other two had gone for some softer option but who could blame them. **(Alex Channon)**

1970-71 EUROPEAN CUP WINNERS' CUP

MANCHESTER CITY 1   LINFIELD 0

Goal Scorer: Bell
European Cup Winners' Cup
First Round – First Leg, Wednesday 16 September 1970
Maine Road, Manchester
Attendance: 25,184

City Team:
Corrigan, Book, Pardoe, Doyle, Booth, Oakes, Summerbee, Bell, Lee, Young, Towers

PRESS VIEW

Little Linfield, the Irish no hopers held the mighty Manchester City for 83 minutes, only a late Colin Bell goal saved City from humiliation. The Irishmen can look forward to what promises to be one of the most stirring battles in their history. City simply did not know how to break down the Irish. (*Daily Mirror*)

City frustrated by gallant Linfield

This was a tactical triumph for Billy Bingham and his red shirted stalwarts. They frustrated, confused and all but confounded the Cup holders, refusing to allow a series of extraordinary escapes to affect their composure throughout a hectic 90 minutes.

Their methods may not have always conformed to the laws, but it would be churlish to deprive them of the credit for what is in fact a moral victory in this first leg.

Seven minutes from time a long ball from Oakes was misjudged by the tall McAllister, his one error of the night and Bell hit a close range goal. A one goal lead is perhaps a poor start at a packed and partisan Windsor Park, but Linfield now know they have a chance of victory and must in consequence, come out and attack.

LINFIELD MANAGEMENT VIEW

I feel we are fit enough to work hard for 90 minutes. Facing a top English side is always a tough hurdle for an Irish League Club, but we shall not be overawed by City's great reputation. I think that they might well be surprised at our high standard of fitness. **(Billy Bingham)**

This is a higher grade of football, much higher, but if we get a good result in the away game then our hopes will be raised for the return leg at Windsor Park. **(Billy Bingham)**

LINFIELD SUPPORTER'S TALE

As a fresh-faced schoolboy from the Shankill, I managed to persuade my father to include me in the party that travelled to Maine Road for the first leg, along with 1,500 supporters, and what a memorable occasion it was. Following an overnight journey on the Heysham boat, we travelled via Morecambe, to Manchester.

City were a team oozing with talent, Joe Corrigan in goal, veteran Tony Book at right back and the stylish Glyn Pardoe on the left, then there was Oakes, Lee, Summerbee and Bell. Yes it was a formidable line up.

But the Blues (of Linfield) turned in one of their impressive away performances of the European stage. It was Colin Bell who hit the winning goal only minutes from the final whistle to save City's blushes on the night, sending hordes of Bluemen home across the Irish Sea in a jubilant mood. **(Alex Mills, Ulster)**

LINFIELD 2   MANCHESTER CITY 1

Goal Scorer: Lee   (City win on away goals)
European Cup Winners' Cup
First Round – Second Leg, Wednesday 30 September 1970
Windsor Park, Belfast
Attendance: 21,000 to 24,000

City Team:
Corrigan, Book, Pardoe, Doyle, Jeffries, Oakes, Summerbee, Bell, Lee (Bowyer), Young, Towers

PRESS VIEW

Manchester City finished their tie at Linfield defending desperately the slimmest of advantages. They won on an away goal after a 2-1 defeat by the Irish part timers. The match was twice held up while bottles were cleared from the City goal after Corrigan had been hit on the ankle. (*Daily Mail*)

Manchester City stuttered and spluttered through to the second round of the European Cup Winners' Cup and were pushed all the way by an enterprising Linfield side. (*Manchester Evening News*)

Windsor Park was packed to the rafters for the return game and again City fielded their strongest side and they appeared to have killed the tie when Francis Lee shot them into a lead inside the first 15 minutes.

However Linfield were not to be intimidated. Billy Millen shot low past Joe Corrigan for the equaliser before the break and the international venue exploded with noise when the lanky winger did it again to grab a winning goal.

It was one of the most memorable nights in the clubs European history. **(Alex Mills, Ulster)**

> ### Irish shame City but Lee's 'Double' goal swings tie
> A Francis Lee goal after six minutes put Manchester City, the holders, into the second round of the European Cup-Winner's Cup at Windsor Park, Belfast last night, but City lost the match to these Irish League part timers, and with it went a large part of their reputation.
>
> Despite the home sides triumph and the 2-2 aggregate scoreline, Lee's goal, since it was scored away, counted double and saved City.
>
> Undoubtedly, City looked the more polished and there were times when they looked as though they could outplay Linfield, but that mood was only temporary and their frustration became evident by the number of times they could do nothing else but pass the ball back to Corrigan from just inside their own half.
>
> It was a bad night for City, but a great one for Irish football.

MANAGEMENT VIEW

If that's what they call an easy tie, give me a really tough one any time. **(Joe Mercer)**

SUPPORTERS' VIEWS

Linfield are out, but this is one of the greatest moments in the footballing history of this country. **(An Irish critic)**

Belfast in the early '70s was a grim place, with bombs going off every other day, barbed wire and gun emplacements all over the place. So it was with some trepidation that I boarded the ferry from Heysham, but was soon at ease when we found Mooney's bar in Belfast, it was not that big, but big enough to get a dozen or so City fans in.

Linfield held the game at Windsor Park, so when we entered the ground we were a little taken back by the high fence and heavy policing and a well-aimed bottle that hit Joe Corrigan and laid him out for five minutes did little to ease the sense of intimidation.

At one stage we were thinking of relying on the bottle to demand a replay as Linfield led 2-1 and looked like scoring another. But it finished 2-1 and City sneaked through on the away goal and we were thankful. **(MCFC Supporter)**

HONVED 0   MANCHESTER CITY 1

Goal Scorer: Lee
European Cup Winners' Cup
Second Round – First Leg, Wednesday 21 October 1970
Kispest Stadium
Attendance: 10,000 to 14,000

City Team:
Corrigan, Book, Pardoe, Doyle, Heslop, Jeffries, Summerbee, Bell, Lee, Hill, Towers

PRESS VIEW

It was the complete performance in every respect except the final flourish. The killer punch, which might have produced four, five or maybe more goals, was missing, but that was all. There was still enough football stemming from elegant City to satisfy the most discerning continental connoisseur. (*Daily Mirror*)

City scored one goal and Honved will swear forever they got an equaliser, but this is immaterial in the context of City's eight goal chances in the first half and seven in the second. This might have been a record score by an away team in the first leg of this tournament. (*Daily Telegraph*)

It was a brilliant performance by City, who on this form look capable of becoming the first club to win this trophy twice in succession. They took control of the game from the start giving a splendid display of cultured attacking football. (*Sun*)

City took over almost completely. They were given space and time in which to work and their midfield dominance was never in question. Perhaps it was a little too easy because City should have scored before they actually did. (*Guardian*)

Since Honved created only three scoring chances to more than a dozen by City. I have no doubt at all that the Manchester side will make their way through into the next round of their defence of the European trophy. (*Daily Mail*)

Glimpses of high quality skill allied to aggressive running saw Manchester City probe and pound Honved into submission in the Kispest stadium. It could have been five following one of City's best ever displays in the European arena. (*Daily Express*)

Bell's injury is the only damper to super show
Mature Manchester City flew back home from here last night with the satisfaction of men who had given their most cultured performance yet in Europe.

Although they had gained only a single goal win against Honved in the first leg of the Cup-Winner's Cup tie, they towered above the Hungarian Army Team in skill and creative control. Their goal was long overdue when Francis Lee scored with such flair and assurance in the 65th minute, and yet they were lucky nine minutes from the finish not to have to settle for a draw that would have flattered the Hungarians, after Spanish referee Rafael Medina ruled that the ball had not gone over the line in a desperate scramble in their goalmouth. Angry Hungarian fans were in no doubt at all and it was fortunate that the referee's peace of mind that he didn't understand their taunts.

City's goal was the end product of one of the most superbly executed set pieces. Colin Bell took a free kick 30 yards out and steered it out to Mike Summerbee on the left of the defensive screen, Summerbee pushed it left to right and Lee swept on to it majestically to crash it into the net.

CITY PLAYER & MANAGEMENT QUOTES

Some managers prefer a home tie initially to build a commanding lead. I would rather go away first and then face the second leg knowing exactly the task that faces you. **(Malcolm Allison)**

I'm sure they can be a much better side. Just because we are leading by one goal, it would be a mistake to assume that it is all over. It's not over by a long chalk... **(Tony Book)**

MANCHESTER CITY 2   HONVED 0

Goal Scorers: Bell, Lee
European Cup Winners' Cup
Second Round – Second Leg, Wednesday 4 November 1970
Maine Road, Manchester
Attendance: 28,770

City Team:
Corrigan, Book, Pardoe, Doyle, Heslop, Oakes, Summerbee, Bell, Lee, Hill, Towers

PRESS VIEW

Manchester City face a supreme test of temperament at Maine Road tonight. They revealed a cultured poise and growing maturity in the first leg of the European Cup Winners' Cup tie against Honved in Budapest two weeks ago. Now a searching spotlight will be focused on their ability to shield the one goal lead they built in the first leg against a crack Hungarian army side. (*Manchester Evening News*)

Manchester City the Cup Winners' Cup holders stormed through against Honved with goals from Bell and Lee. (*Daily Mail*)

Manchester City emerged as saturated supermen when effortlessly thrusting aside a double obstacle on their way to the quarter final of the European Cup Winners' Cup. They shattered a Honved side that lacked both physical challenge and conviction in their own ability, but what is more important is they conquered almost farcical conditions, in a water logged pitch to win. (*Manchester Evening News*)

Manchester City warned Europe last night with a thoroughly professional performance that they intend to hang onto the Cup Winners' Cup. They provided magnificent football on a morass Maine Road pitch topped by two inches of continuous rain and completely outclassed the Hungarians. (*Daily Mirror*)

Once again the sadly outclassed Hungarians escaped the anticipated slaughter and this time Manchester City can blame their own climate. (*Daily Telegraph*)

Mercer men plough through mud and rain

Mighty Manchester City powered their way through pouring rain and a paddy field of a pitch last night into the quarter-finals of Europe' cup winners.

Their hopelessly inferior and ill equipped rivals from Budapest presented no problems to them compared with the appalling conditions, but City proved themselves the true all purpose, all weather side. It was a dynamic display that did great credit to the resilience and the ruggedness of the British professional.

A goal by one of Honveds arch tormentors Colin Bell set them on their way to their one sided success in the 19th minute when he bored his way through a solid mass of defenders and in the 65th minute the non-stop aggression of his England team mate Francis Lee was justly rewarded when Honved half back Vagi deflected what might well have intended to be a cross rather than a shot into the net.

MANAGEMENT VIEW

Honved were a big name but they were a disappointment on the night when the weather did not help the gate.

You have got to go for goals at home. European competition is worth so much in football and Honved are one of the great names in post war European football. (**Joe Mercer**)

CAPTAIN'S VIEW
We played well in Budapest in the first leg. We are out to play even better tonight. **(Tony Book)**

HONVED VIEW
My players were lost in the heavy going. City rose above it, we had it on our minds and we got worse and worse. **(Kalman Preiner, Honved manager)**

GORNIK ZABRZE 2   MANCHESTER CITY 0
European Cup Winners' Cup
Quarter Final – First Leg, Wednesday 10 March 1971
Stadion Slaski, Chorzow'
Attendance: 100,000

City Team:
Corrigan, Book, Towers, Doyle, Booth, Oakes, Summerbee, Bell, Lee, Young, Jeffries

PRESS VIEW
Manchester City took their out of tune First division form with them into Europe and now stand perilously close to having their last major trophy within sight torn from their grasp. (*Manchester Evening News*)

Gornik, seeking revenge for their defeat by City in last season's final, always looked the stronger and more skilful side and a score of 2-0 adequately reflected their superiority. (*Guardian*)

City's attack is failure as Poles earn advantage
Gorniks' richly deserved two goal lead is not insurmountable in the second leg at Maine Road but unless City can raise their game considerably above this standard their European dreams will be halted. The attack despite the presence together of three England forwards had little pace, no invention and no more fire power than a spent candle. The pitch although clear of snow was frozen in patches and City spent the opening minutes skidding and sliding as Gornik attacked swiftly under a pale freezing sunset. Lubanski struck after 55 minutes when he streaked into the area and glided the ball left footed past Corrigan's unavailing dive.

Five minutes later City's defence was completely stricken by an even better move that let in Wilczek; Corrigan saved the shot but failed to hold the ball.

The miners team had everything from pitch to fanatical crowd in their favour on this emotion charged, bleak cold evening. Another factor is that Gornik on an ice rink pitch revealed they are a formidable and skilful side. (***Daily Express***)

Defensive slackness and a man called Lubanski were the prime reasons for City's heaviest defeat in Europe. Candidly I rate skipper Tony Book and his men fortunate to escape with irreparable harm. (***Daily Mirror***)

Manchester City must now grimly prepare for their toughest ever ordeal since they marched into Europe three years ago, after the near disaster of this quarter final in the hostile Silesian stadium, their chances of surviving in the Cup Winners' Cup are almost as harsh as the deep freeze Polish winter. (***Sun***)

Wonder man Lubanski set Gornik on their way to success in this first leg of the Cup Winners' Cup quarter final with a superb goal after 35 minutes. City do not see the situation as irretrievable, but there will have to be a striking transformation in the next two weeks if they are to hang on to the trophy. (***Daily Mail***)

SUPPORTERS' TALES

One of our regular visits back to my parent's homeland (visa pending), coincidentally clashed with City's European clash against Gornik. My aunt put us up and unbeknown to us, my uncle had four tickets through his son (Kris), for the Polish end, which was great news for my father and brother who were big City supporters.

Gorniks Slask (Sliesla) stadium, which in those days made up part of a theme park 'Happy Town', was a vast open ground and we were sitting on long wooden benches with the Polish International squad sat behind us. As to the game I can remember a vociferous crowd politely applaud the silky skills of City but were in raptures when Gornik scored two goals.

After the game had finished I witnessed a coach being trashed outside the supporters' club, but I can't tell you who was doing the damage or to whom the coach belonged to as my aunty dragged me past as we made our way to the players' lounge where we gained access with no problem. It contained a mixture of players from the Polish International squad, fans from both clubs and officials, all stood around talking in a vibrant atmosphere. I got the opportunity to meet some of the players but was awe struck to ask for any autographs. Well I was only ten at the time. (**Kasha Edwards, Victoria Park**)

There are six of us on this trip all armed with our short stay visas from the Polish embassy. We sailed out of Harwich and then caught a train to Warsaw and then onto Krakow to check into the Hotel Orbis.

City fans started to arrive from the airport and we negotiated with the couriers for tickets. They had lots of spares as half the City fans on the trip turned out to be Poles taking a cheap chance to visit relatives in Poland. The hotel staff said we could go on the coach to the ground but would have to charge us 50 Zlotys. On arrival at the ground, we found the pitch had been cleared of all the snow but not the seats and the terraces were still frozen.

In the ground we met 'Big George', a giant Pole, who sat in front of us. He warmed himself up by picking up a bench and whirling it round his head. Then he offered us some vodka before starting a fire to keep himself warm.

I knew they had been on a sunshine tour to Spain, but I thought their legs could not be as brown as that, until dawned on me that they were wearing tights. (Francis Lee reflecting on the cold after a vast army of 800 workmen had maintained a round the clock vigil, to keep the pitch clears of snow.)

MANCHESTER CITY 2   GORNIK ZABRZE 0
Goal Scorers: Mellor, Doyle
European Cup Winners' Cup
Quarter Final – Second Leg, Wednesday 24 March 1971
Maine Road, Manchester
Attendance: 31,950

City Team: Healey, Connor, Towers, Doyle, Booth, Donachie, Jeffries, Bell, Lee, Young (Mann), Mellor (Bowyer)

PRESS VIEW
Manchester City live to fight another day in Copenhagen, taking the redoubtable Polish side, Gornik, into extra time to draw 2-2. (***Daily Mirror***)

Manchester City tried everyone's nerves at Maine Road. Starting 2-0 down they fielded an unfamiliar team with four young reserves, sheer effort wore the experienced Gornik down and City were level on aggregate by midway through the second half, the goals coming from Mellor and Doyle. Then the effort took its toll and even though half an hour of extra time they could not score the winner. (***Daily Mail***)

Magnificent Manchester City stood by Joe Mercers pledge to the letter. They smashed into Gornik with an explosion in a glittering tension jammed cup winners' cup quarter final, on a night of torrential rain and heat hugging emotion. (***Manchester Evening News***)

MANAGEMENT & PLAYER VIEW
This is the most exciting game Manchester City have been involved in during the last five or six years. It's full of drama we are two goals down, to one of the best sides in Europe. The atmosphere could be electric, if we score in the first twenty minutes, then

there is everything to play for. We have the courage to win this one and that can be our only possible approach. **(Malcolm Allison)**

Whatever happens tonight, you can be sure it won't be the result of a miracle. To come back in a game like this you have to have skill and dedication and we have that. If we can survive this test considering all our injury problems, there is no reason to doubt we can achieve a great result. **(Joe Mercer)**

Four days after making my debut, I played in the European Cup Winners' Cup and scored, so it was really a great start. **(Ian Mellor)**

GORNIK ZABRZE 1 MANCHESTER CITY 3

Goal Scorers: Booth, Young, Lee
European Cup Winners' Cup
Quarter Final – Replay, Wednesday 31 March 1971
Idraetsparken Stadium, Copenhagen
Attendance: 12,100

City Team: Healey, Connor, Towers, Doyle, Booth, Donachie, Jeffries, Bell, Lee, Young, Hill

Gornik's president, Earnest Wyra, demanded that City's players be tested for drugs, after his claims that the side had taken drugs during the second leg and he wanted to see them punished.

I don't want you wasting your energy by getting worked up over this business. You must ignore this kind of thing, no matter how distasteful it may sound and concentrate everything on beating Gornik in the play off. **(Joe Mercer)**

Those words got home all right but first City had to bow to authority and agree to submit to the dope tests, but this was not the first time the Gornik club had asked for a dope test to be made on players. Twelve months earlier, they asked officials to conduct tests on the players of Italian side, Roma.

After beating Gornik in Copenhagen, it then took another hour to prove that City had done it legally as Colin Bell, David Connor and Derek Jeffries were subjected to sixty minutes of pure farce as they tried in vain to give urine samples.

MANAGEMENT VIEW

I'm a proud man tonight. I would have been proud if our top strength team had pulled off such a performance but with all the boys in the side it was superb. They can go forward to meet Chelsea with confidence. They gave me all I wanted. **(Malcolm Allison)**

City make dopes out of Gornik

Cool, calm and cultured Manchester City coasted through last night to their most impressive away victory in Europe. Their second defeat of their Polish rivals within a week left Graceless Gornik, the club that had accused them of using drugs, in no doubt at all who were the masters.

On an immaculate pitch which had been covered by their painstaking Danish hosts until half an hour before kick-off, City turned the tie into something almost as sedate as a studious game of chess.

Neil Young, the marksman who has struck telling blows on many big occasions for City and centre half Tommy Booth gave their side a two goal lead by the interval, and after ace striker Lubanski had scored for Gornik in their one brief spell of determination in the second half, England forward Francis Lee crashed in their clincher in the 65th minute.

City's impeccable display would have been a credit even to the top strength team that conquered Europe last season.

CHELSEA 1   MANCHESTER CITY 0

European Cup Winners' Cup
Semi Final – First Leg, Wednesday 14 April 1971
Stamford Bridge
Attendance: 45,595

City Team: Corrigan, Book, Connor, Towers, Booth, Donachie, Johnson, Hill, Lee, Young, Mann
Subs: Healey (GK), Carter, Brennan, Heslop, Mellor

PRESS VIEW

The unquenchable spirit of players who recently would hardly have considered themselves possible selection for such a crucial match was of inestimable value to City's chances of retaining the trophy. Now they have a precious breathing space of two weeks to prepare for the return at Maine Road. (***Daily Mirror***)

The remodelled side came within striking distance of achieving a goalless draw. One mistake in the 47th minute let in Derek Smethurst to provide the FA Cup holders with the fragile thread they must dangle by. (***Daily Express***)

City's defensive intentions were made obvious with seven passes back to keeper Corrigan inside the first six minutes. But a scrappy Chelsea were making it easier for them. (***Sun***)

Although they conceded a goal to Chelsea in the 47th minute the gap is not nearly as great as they must have feared it would be when three senior players joined an already lengthy casualty list. (***Daily Telegraph***)

Chelsea started with the bold and aggressive manner of men who believed they might win by a cricket score, but for all their breathless effort, they found themselves pitted against fearless foes that lacked nothing in spirit or determination. (*Daily Mail*)

Incredible City

Incredible Manchester City bravely shrugged off their injury burden and achieved a result at Chelsea last night for which few teams in their unhappy plight would even have dared to hope.

They lost the first leg of the Cup-Winners' Cup semi-final at Stamford Bridge by a single goal, but they won the profound admiration of countless London soccer supporters by their courageous struggle. Admittedly they lived dangerously in a punishing battle in which the latest of their make shift teams was subjected to fearsome pressure.

Chelsea started with the bold and aggressive manner of men who believed they might win by a cricket score. But for all their breathless effort, they found themselves pitted against fearless foes that lacked nothing in spirit or determination even though they went into the tie without six of their injured senior stars.

The goal for which Chelsea had to settle was scored by Derek Smethurst a minute after the interval.

SUPPORTER'S VIEW

The semi-final of the 1971 Cup Winners' Cup paired City against Chelsea. The first leg was at Stamford Bridge. This was a game that on face value City were able to win, especially as they had thrashed Chelsea 3-0 at the Bridge in the FA Cup in January, but and there is always a but when talking about City, we were at the time having an injury crisis, two thirds of the famous three of Lee, Bell and Summerbee were injured, only Francis Lee being fit for the first leg. Colin Bell in particular would be missed as he had almost singularly destroyed Chelsea in the FA Cup meeting. We were also missing Mike Doyle and Glynn Pardoe.

The trip to the capital by many City fans was by use of a football special train to Euston and then by tube to Chelsea. At the time the tube was new to us Northerners, which resulted in a party of four having to follow a City fan we knew from Eccles and then arranging to meet after the game to lead us back to Euston, sad but true.

Eventually we arrived at the ground to find we were seated in the North stand. A stand built on stilts, a real ramshackle excuse for a stand, a stand that vibrated every time supporters cheered. Safety of sports ground regulators never inspected a stand like that. It was in fact demolished a few years later.

The game itself started and not unexpectantly and considering the injury crisis, it was a back to the wall job, a real defensive slog. Chelsea though for all their dominance could not get a break through. So as the first half drew to a close we were quite pleased at the 0-0 scoreline, after all the second leg at Maine Road was to come.

The second half commenced, but after only two minutes, Derek Smethurst, ironically a late Chelsea team change, scored from close range. We now obviously feared the worse with another forty-three minutes to play. Strangely it did not happen that way. Chelsea huffed and puffed and had all the control but could not increase their advantage. Big Joe Corrigan was having an excellent game, but he was to be sadly missed for the second leg at Maine Road. After a torrid ninety minutes were up, we were not to displeased, surely 1-0 could be turned over at Maine Road, when some of our star players would return from injury. **(Roland Griffin, RIP)**

MANCHESTER CITY 0   CHELSEA 1

European Cup Winners' Cup
Semi Final – Second Leg, Wednesday 28 April 1971
Maine Road, Manchester
Attendance: 43,663

City Team: Healey, Book, Connor, Towers, Heslop, Jeffries, Summerbee (Carter), Lee, Bowyer, Young, Johnson (Donachie)

PRESS VIEW

Clubs who between them had eleven players injured and unable to compete played this important match. (*Guardian*)

What remained of Chelsea's best squad last night scattered the few first teamers left to Manchester City and reached the final of the European Cup Winners' Cup. (*Daily Mail*)

Chelsea's enviable strength in depth saw them triumphantly through an injury crisis and onto the final. (*Daily Mirror*)

It was a gamble that failed for Manchester City on a sad night that their crippling toll of injuries finally caught up with them. (*Manchester Evening News*)

The night City kids cracked
It was a gamble that failed for Manchester City on the sad night that their crippling toll of injuries finally caught up with them.

> Joe Mercer dealt two half fit men an inexperienced boy from his depleted pack only to find polished and professional Chelsea holding all the aces that firmly trumped City's brave bid to keep the Cup Winners Cup.
>
> Mike Summerbee and Derek Jeffries were clearly not capable of coping with the demands of a testing European semi-final so soon after injury and the immature Jeffrey Johnson looked totally out of his depth.

MANAGEMENT QUOTES

It's a pity this all England semi-final could not have been avoided, but it still means a good English club will reach the final, whatever the result tonight. **(Joe Mercer)**

I was disappointed in the attitude of the players towards the game. They were afraid before they even started and you should never be afraid. They did not really try to win. I have never seen a Manchester City team go into a big match like that. It looked as if they were playing for a draw. **(Malcolm Allison)**

PLAYER Q&A

JOE CORRIGAN

Manchester City playing record
1967–1982
603 Games

What is your most vivid memory of playing in Europe?
Winning the European Cup Winners' Cup in Vienna against Gornik.

Did you prefer the home legs or the away legs, and why?
Home Legs, as the Manchester City supporters were something special.

Who was the most difficult opponent you faced?
They were all good players.

What was the funniest incident you can remember, or will admit to?
Being stuck in a lift in our hotel before a UEFA Cup match.

What was the food like abroad?
Reasonable to good, the only difficulty was in Eastern Europe where we had to take our own food and chef.

Whose was the most passionate support you played in front of?
Not a European game, but Celtic.

Did any fellow City players have a fear of flying, hate foreign food or was a real grouch at dealing with foreigners?
Arthur Mann hated flying and had to take tablets to calm down before a trip.

Was playing in Europe more important than the domestic game?
No.

How did you feel once the City side you were playing for was knocked out of Europe?
Sick.

If there was one thing you could change about your European adventures with City, what would it be?
The team that played against Borussia for the two legs in the UEFA Cup, we were too inexperienced for the situation.

MIKE SUMMERBEE

Manchester City playing record
1965–1974
452 Games
68 Goals

What is your most vivid memory of playing in Europe?
Playing in Turkey, which was very difficult.

Did you prefer the home legs or the away legs, and why?
It made no difference.

Who was the most difficult opponent you faced?
Paul Brietner.

What was the funniest incident you can remember, or will admit to?
I cannot remember.

What was the food like abroad?
Okay.

Whose was the most passionate support you played in front of?
Not a European game but Barcelona.

Did any fellow City players have a fear of flying, hate foreign food or was a real grouch at dealing with foreigners?
Yes Stan Bowles and Arthur Mann.

Was playing in Europe more important than the domestic game?
No

How did you feel once the City side you were playing for was knocked out of Europe?
We won the trophy.

If there was one thing you could change about your European adventures with City, what would it be?
There is nothing I would change.

FRANCIS LEE

Manchester City playing record
1967–1974
340 Games
148 Goals

What is your most vivid memory of playing in Europe?
Winning the European Cup Winners' Cup in 1970.

Did you prefer the home legs or the away legs, and why?
Home Legs, but away Legs were great for international experience.

Who was the most difficult opponent you faced?
Quite a few, but their names elude me.

What was the funniest incident you can remember, or will admit to?
When we told Joe Mercer that a Portuguese British Airways engineer sat alongside was a hijacker.

What was the food like abroad?
Iron Curtain and Eastern Europe it was terrible, elsewhere just OK to very good, occasionally.

Whose was the most passionate support you played in front of?
Fenerbahçe (Turkey).

Did any fellow City players have a fear of flying, hate foreign food or was a real grouch at dealing with foreigners?
Several feared flying and most hated the food.

Was playing in Europe more important than the domestic game?
No.

How did you feel once the City side you were playing for was knocked out of Europe?
In the European Cup very disappointed but provided you had a fair deal (which was very unusual) it was quite acceptable.

If there was one thing you could change about your European adventures with City, what would it be?
Winning the European Cup.

1970-71 ANGLO ITALIAN CUP

BOLOGNA 1   MANCHESTER CITY 0

Anglo-Italian Cup
First Round – First Leg, Wednesday 2 September 1970
Stadio Comunale
Attendance: 25,000 to 28,000

City Team: Corrigan, Book, Pardoe, Doyle, Booth, Oakes, Summerbee, Bell, Lee, Young, Towers
Subs: Mulhearn (GK), Jeffries, Hill

MANAGEMENT VIEW

England and Italy still possess the greatest strength of any soccer playing countries in Europe, but while we attack they defend and tonight I want to prove that our attacking methods are the better of the two. (**Malcolm Allison**)

PRESS VIEW

Manchester City were beaten 1-0 by Bologna in Italy last night in the first leg of the Anglo Italian Cup. (*Daily Mirror*)

Manchester City went to Italy for a challenge match between the League Cup holders of the two countries. They fielded a strong side but played without much enthusiasm and were beaten 1-0. (*Daily Mail*)

Bologna proved to be a lively and skilful side which City failed miserably to reach even a standard level of performance in either defence, midfield or attack. (*Daily Express*)

This must rank as one of City's most irritating and disappointing performances in European conflict since their first disastrous attempt in the champions cup two years ago. (*Daily Mirror*)

City, Kings of Europe in the Cup Winners' Cup last season, played like plodding peasants last night. (*Daily Mail*)

This display, on a warm sultry evening, was the most disappointing I have seen from City in Europe and they did not seem to have the right attitude or aptitude for the game. (**Denis Lowe**, *Daily Telegraph*)

Manchester City show little zest

The powerful, punishing approach which has made Manchester City such devasting cup fighters was missing in the Stadio Comunale here last night when Bologna, Italian champions on three occasions, won the first leg of the Anglo Italian league Cup Winners Cup by a third minute goal from their international forward Franco Rizzo.

This display on a warm sultry evening was the most disappointing I have seen from City in Europe and they did not seem to have the right attitude or appetite for the game. There were some notable exceptions such as the ever industrious Francis Lee, Mike Doyle and the young sweeper Tony Towers.

Lee, his blue shirt stamped with the sweat of determination and effort, did not spare himself and he and Glyn Pardoe were close to an equalising goal with second half headers. Joe Corrigan however had to make several useful saves and one felt that Bologna could have taken a more decisive lead to Maine Road in three weeks' time.

The goal that put City behind for the first time in six matches this season came before many of the 25,000 spectators had settled down. Bologna split the defence in the third minute with a sharp middle thrust in which Towers and Booth were beaten. Gregori linked up with Savoldi for Rizzo to score with a left footed shot from 16 yards. Corrigan perhaps unsighted was late to go down as the ball went to his left and entered the net just inside the upright.

With City unaccountably slow and unimaginative, Bologna continued to play speedy and artistic football while City continued to be below their normal standard with their distribution and running off the ball incredibly poor.

Doyle's desire to improve matters in the second half was emphasised when he provided fair chances for Lee and Pardoe whose headers finished off target and then City had cause to thank Corrigan for keeping out attempts by Rizzo and the ever dangerous Savoldi.

MANCHESTER CITY 2   BOLOGNA 2

Goal Scorers: Heslop, Lee
Anglo-Italian Cup
First Round – Second Leg, Wednesday 23 September 1970
Maine Road, Manchester
Attendance: 25,843

City Team:
Corrigan, Book, Pardoe, Doyle, Heslop, Oakes, Hill, Bell, Lee, Young, Towers (Summerbee)
Subs: Mulhearn (GK), Jeffries, Bowyer, Carrodus

PRESS VIEW

Cup fighters Manchester City met their masters when Bologna gained a 2-2 draw at Maine Road to win the Anglo-Italian Cup in a game which often threatened a free for all. The Manchester players did not file out to receive their medals. (*Daily Mail*)

City threatened many times in the second half to overpower the Bologna defence but again the Italians broke out at a blistering pace to shock them. (*Daily Mail*)

The Italians, after shocking City by taking the lead, dropped back into the predictable defensive show once City had drawn level. (*Sun*)

City became the victims of their own impatience and fell repeatedly into the traps set so expertly by a defence who had been well schooled in the arts of 'catenaccio' in Italy. (*Daily Mirror*)

Undoubtedly City can make a case for victory. A refused penalty and a disallowed goal by Francis Lee add to the dossier. (*Daily Express*)

Rugged Italians Make City pay for their errors

Bologna carried off the Anglo Italian Cup at Maine Road last night after a stormy and bruising second leg tie against Manchester City, and it appears that this new competition will do little to promote friendship and increase understanding between two countries whose idea of football are at time poles apart.

The Italians followed up their one goal home victory with a draw, winning 3-2 on aggregate. Bologna's scorers were Perani and Savoldi and City who created four times as many opportunities had to be satisfied with two equalisers from Lee and Heslop.

If Lee and Bell, two brave and belligerent forwards, had been given better support and if more of the close range chances had been taken, there would have been another piece of silverware in the Maine Road boardroom. Vavassori, a capable if harassed goalkeeper, played his part in Bologna's success, with a number of remarkable saves particularly from Lee, Oakes and Young. Hill, Lee, Bell and Doyle all missed when it seemed easier to score

Things looked ugly for a time towards the end of the first half when players on both sides became involved in petty vendettas. The needling, niggling tactics of the Italians were answered with hasty retaliation on City's part.

All in the entire match had contained some fine purposeful football but the clash of temperaments was always too close to the surface.

1972-73 UEFA CUP

MANCHESTER CITY 2   VALENCIA CF 2

Goal Scorers: Mellor, Marsh
UEFA Cup
First Round – First Leg, Wednesday 13 September 1972
Maine Road, Manchester
Attendance: 21,698

City Team: Corrigan (Healey), Jeffries, Donachie, Doyle, Booth, Oakes, Mellor, Bell, Marsh, Lee, Towers
Subs: Barrett, Davies, Hill, Carrodus

PRESS VIEW

Manchester City cling by their fingertips to a place in Europe. They are down but by no means out, after producing their most impressive performance of the season. They tore into a talented, tough Valencia but at the end of a rip roaring first leg, could only emerge with a 2-2 draw.

A half empty stadium symbolised Manchester City's slow start to the season, but with Malcolm Allison's men showing some of their former flair and aggression. The missing thousands made a mistake in choosing this game for their protest. (*Daily Mirror*)

The sweet scent of the big occasion brought Manchester City out of their slump in an exhilarating all action thriller of a cup tie. (*Daily Mail*)

Quick exit stares City in the face

Unhappy Manchester City created the chances at Maine Road to have strolled into the UEFA cup second round, yet instead are faced with elimination in Valencia in two weeks by a team short of neither skill nor fire.

Last night's encounter, touching occasional peaks, was loaded with action throughout and it must be feared that, football apart, the embers of violence have been fanned for the return leg which may find City's tactics spiced with desperation.

Valencia's centre back Anton went off early needing four stitches and subsequently Sergio, Sol and Adorno were booked. The satisfaction of the result is not regarded by the Spaniards' as compensation for, in their eyes, some injustices.

For City there is the frustration that from easily their best performance of a troubled season they have gained no advantage. An inch here or there could have turned two goals into six, on top of which they conceded two when twice caught napping.

In front of a disappointing 21,000 crowd City's problems last night were a back line vulnerable to the isolated fast counter-attack and in their own front line, too much skill rather than too little. They were off to a fine if fortunate start when Melendez, the Spanish goalkeeper, foolishly went off on a dribble that ended with him losing the ball to Mellor who as the players fell, was first on his feet to put the ball in an empty net. For the rest of the first half City attacked persistently but their finish lacked refinement. Marsh had a looping centre cleared off the line. Bell and Lee several times went close but just on half time Valdez punished appalling hesitation between Booth, Oakes and Corrigan to level the score.

Worse was to follow when early in the second half Valdez and Sergio sliced through a ponderous defence to put Adorno clear on the right from where he beat Corrigan with a low shot.

Now City were in serious trouble, relieved only a little when Marsh banged in their second with half an hour to go.

VALENCIA CF 2   MANCHESTER CITY 1

Goal Scorer: Marsh

UEFA Cup

First Round – Second Leg, Wednesday 27 September 1972
Mastella Stadium
Attendance: 35,000 to 54,000

City Team: Healey, Book, Barrett, Doyle, Booth (Mellor), Oakes, Summerbee, Bell, Marsh, Lee, Towers
Subs: Dunlop (GK), Clarke, Carrodus, Brennan

PRESS VIEW

Manchester City's pride, almost totally extinguished by weeks of first division adversity was rekindled in Valencia, but the Blues most scintillating performance of the season was insufficient for them to break through a barrier of despair that remains flying across their path of progress. (*Daily Express*)

Manchester City may be bottom of the first division but they put up a tremendous fight before bowing out of Europe, for 70% of a rousing UEFA Cup tie, they had a crack Valencia team on the rack. (*Daily Mirror*)

Two superb goals from Valencias ace marksmen Valdez and Quino blasted Manchester City out of Europe last night. Even though the English side had given their Spanish rivals a tremendous fight in a tough battle in which five players were booked, the big home crowd lashed their side into a storming second half surge of power. (*Daily Mail*)

City miss their chance

Two crisp goals in nine minutes not long from the end cut short Manchester City's voyage in the UEFA Cup before they had even reached the first port, and now they are left to pick up the bits as best they can in the league.

It was a sad exit, for City had been on the offensive for most of the first hour against a Valencia side which, with brilliant forwards, strangely decided to defend their away goals from the 2-2 draw at Maine Road. This tactical decision by manager Alfredo Di Stefano nearly handed the tie to City, for they kept pushing forward and had their chances and Bell missed an open goal in the 33rd minute. That was a critical turning point. A goal then would surely have put City in a powerful position, psychologically and tactically but instead their initiative waned from the start of the second half. The blow City feared came in the 71st minute when Valdez put through by Quiono beat Healey with a low shot.

Vainly City threw themselves back into attack and Booth had two headers cleared off the line, but with 10 minutes to go a scorching shot by Quino from 20 yards left Healey helpless.

Sergio hit the bar from five yards as City began to founder and Marsh's overhead kick to give City their goal in the last minute was a defiant gesture that came too late.

PLAYER QUOTES

We are not going to Spain a beaten side. We are going to do our dardnest to swing the game our way and salvage some self respect after our disastrous start to the season. **(Tony Book)**

With Alan Oakes fit, it does not look as though I will have to turn out but I shall be one of the substitutes and this alone made it a sleepless night for me I hardly got a winks sleep. **(Jeff Clarke)**

Clarke, is a big strong lad, who could well go places, he has got a few rough edges. I have played with him in the reserves and I can assure you there will be no doubts about his abilities. **(Tony Book)**

PLAYER Q&A

IAN MELLOR

Manchester City playing record
1970–1972
50 Games
10 Goals

What is your most vivid memory of playing in Europe?
Scoring my first goal for Manchester City.

Did you prefer the home legs or the away legs, and why?
Home Legs as every player plays better at home.

Who was the most difficult opponent you faced?
None, as I scored in both the European games I played in.

What was the funniest incident you can remember, or will admit to?
Being drug tested and not being able to produce a sample.

What was the food like abroad?
Okay, as we stayed in the best hotels.

Whose was the most passionate support you played in front of?
Manchester City's.

Did any fellow City players have a fear of flying, hate foreign food or was a real grouch at dealing with foreigners?
Arthur Mann hated flying and could only get on a plane if he was drunk.

Was playing in Europe more important than the domestic game?
In a way, yes, as the matches had a bit more of a buzz to them.

How did you feel once the City side you were playing for was knocked out of Europe?
Sick, no one likes losing.

If there was one thing you could change about your European adventures with City, what would it be?
Nothing really as two goals in two games is something I am very proud of.

1976-77 UEFA CUP

MANCHESTER CITY 1   JUVENTUS 0

Goal Scorer: Kidd
UEFA Cup
First Round – First Leg, Wednesday 15 September 1976
Maine Road, Manchester
Attendance: 36,955

> **City Team:**
> Corrigan, Docherty, Donachie, Doyle, Watson, Conway, Barnes (Power), Kidd, Royle, Hartford, Tueart
> Subs: Macrae (GK), Clements, Booth, Lester

PRESS VIEW

Manchester City had to be content at Maine Road last night with something rather less than the three goal lead with which ideally they had hoped to mark their return to European soccer after an absence of years. (*Daily Telegraph*)

City have it all to do but I am convinced they can conquer the odds by staying bold. (*Daily Mirror*)

This tie will not be over until the second leg.
　We only got the one goal lead which Juventus were happy with. The goal was just before half time, which is a great time to score, but we could not break them down in the second half. They just got behind the ball.
　We are in the right mood for what will undoubtedly be a difficult game. Italian teams are hard to break down when they play away from home. We have worked hard for the last two years to get back into Europe and our aim now is to stay here. (**Tony Book**)

JUVENTUS 2   MANCHESTER CITY 0

UEFA Cup
First Round – Second Leg, Wednesday 29 September 1976
Stadio Comunale, Turin
Attendance: 55,000

> **City Team:**
> Corrigan, Docherty, Donachie, Doyle, Watson, Booth, Keegan (Lester), Kidd, Royle, Hartford, Tueart
> Subs: Macrae (GK), Power, Owen, Clements

PRESS VIEW

The outstretched fingers and swift reflexes of keeper Dino Zoff were all that stood between Manchester City and a sensational if undeserved victory. (*Daily Mirror*)

Manchester City are out of the UEFA cup and no one can complain. (*Daily Mail*)

Manchester City went out of the UEFA Cup, last night after another depressing illustration of the incompatibility of English and Italian teams. Juventus by far the sharper and more creative side deserved to go through. (*Daily Express*)

They kicked ten bells out of us, unbelievable. We were very inexperienced. Very, very poor in that European tie. No real steal, no European steel. (**Dennis Tueart**)

City's attacking plan is failure in Turin

Manchester City's plan to attack their way into the second round of the UEFA cup foundered miserably on two goals, one in each half, from Juventus at the huge and intimidating Stadio Comunale last night.

The first goal of the match which City had been so keen to score themselves came from Scirea. Juventus finally battered a way through the City defence. Docherty blocked Scirea's first shot after the Italian had accepted a pass from Causio. When the rebound came back to him, though, the big, powerful defender made no mistake with his second shot and the one that gave Juventus a decisive overall lead was scored in the 69th minute by Boninsegna. He cut short City's return to European soccer after a four year absence by volleying the ball past Corrigan. The plain fact though is that City did not attack Juventus as promised, simply because the adventurous Italians would not let them.

The game was played in pouring rain, but the pitch was in excellent condition at the kick off because it had been protected by plastic sheeting which was rolled up and removed only a few minutes before play started.

1977-78 UEFA CUP

MANCHESTER CITY 2   WIDZEW LODZ 2

Goal Scorers: Barnes, Channon
UEFA Cup
First Round – First Leg, Wednesday 14 September 1977
Maine Road, Manchester
Attendance: 33,695

City Team:
Corrigan, Clements, Donachie, Owen, Watson, Booth, Barnes, Channon, Kidd, Hartford, Keegan (Royle)

On a night of nostalgia for the Polish community of Manchester, many members of the Shrewsbury Street headquarters of the Polish ex-service men's club were asked their view on how they felt Lodz would fair against City.

Lodz of trouble. I think City will win 3-0 but they may have to draw 2-2 in Lodz. I know only a little about this team, they are not so well known even in Poland. There is a good player, Boniek, but they are not so special. (**Leopold Kedzior**)

Not many times have English teams gone to Poland and won. They will not find it easy in Lodz. It will be hard for them away from home, but I think City will win 3-1 at home. (**Leon Jutrzenka**)

I want to go for sentimental reasons. I went to the game when Gornik were at Maine Road. My boy was aged 10 and he shouted for City while I shouted for Gornik. (**Feliks Bartoszak**)

PRESS VIEW

Manchester City surrendered a two goal lead in four minutes last night to leave themselves in a perilous position for the second leg in Poland. (*Daily Mirror*)

Manchester City ignored the warning lights flashed by the red hair of Polish genius Zbigniew Boniek and could pay for it with their life in Europe. (*Daily Mail*)

Willie Donachie was ordered off in the final minute of a niggling UEFA Cup tie at Maine Road, when City surrendered a two goal lead and left them with a lot to do in Poland. (*Daily Telegraph*)

Knife Edge of uncertainty

Manchester City may be top of the First Division but they are bottom of the League so far as Europe is concerned. The Blues UEFA Cup hopes are very much up the pole after a disgraceful first leg performance in which they tossed away a two goal lead and then had humiliation piled on them with Willie Donachie sent off in injury time.

It leaves them precariously balanced on a knife edge of uncertainty when they make the long haul to Poland for the second leg against Widez Lodz, and frankly I can't see City surviving. How can they expect to win in the fury and fire of a passionate Polish stadium when they can't even win on their own ground.

Maine Road last night provided a classic case of City completely underestimating opponents and at the same time vastly experienced professionals allowed themselves to be conned by continental tactics from a side having their first taste of European football. Yet it was City who at times looked the newcomers as they nervously bunched in front of goal seeking the chances to score the goals manager Tony Book had asked for.

City however should not have been in this position, they gave themselves a flying start, Peter Barnes scoring a glorious opening goal after just 10 minutes, but for once City's normally impregnable defence looked suspect under pressure and Lodz scored twice in four minutes, the second from a penalty and only had Mike Channon to thank for his equaliser on 81 minutes.

MANAGEMENT VIEW

We can still do it. We now have got to go over there and play them at their own game. We must try and make it as difficult for them as they did for us. I had set a target of three goals to safeguard us in Poland. The two we got would have been enough but then we threw them away. **(Tony Book)**

After Boniek scored an incensed fan ran towards him. He was found guilty of using threatening and abusive behaviour and banned from Maine Road but City were instructed to erect fencing behind both goals.

When get back home, we will report the attack by the spectator to the proper channels. **(Bronislaw Waligera, Lodz Coach)**

WIDZEW LODZ 0   MANCHESTER CITY 0

(City lost on away goals rule)
UEFA Cup
First Round – Second Leg, Wednesday 28 September 1977
Stadion LKS
Attendance: 40,000

City Team: Corrigan, Doyle (Clements), Power, Owen, Watson, Booth, Barnes, Kidd, Royle, Hartford, Tueart

PRESS VIEW

Joe Royle threw away the sort of chance which will torment him whenever European competition is mentioned and with it went Manchester City's chance of surviving. (*Daily Mirror*)

Manchester City's European ambitions evaporated when Joe Royle's boot met only air in the most critical moment of this fierce UEFA tie. (*Daily Mail*)

I feel disappointed but I was proud of the way the entire team played over the ninety minutes. We just did not get the breaks we deserved. (**Tony Book**)

City's attacking gamble fails in goalless draw

Manchester City a pale ineffective shadow of the side which has raced to the top of the First Division went out of the UEFA cup in dismal fashion yesterday afternoon when Widzew Lodz, bottom of the Polish League, drew 2-2 on aggregate and qualified for the second round because of the goals they scored at Maine Road.

The damage was done in the second half of the first leg when City threw away a two goal lead and enabled the Poles to draw a match in which they should have been beaten convincingly. When City at last showed something of their form after an hour of the second leg, the Poles were content to contain them and settle for a goalless score line.

Yet if the Manchester team were well below their best and woefully short of ideas, they had the best scoring chance in a match which produced very few of them. It came in the 40th minute when Joe Royle, left unchallenged in front of an empty net after Burzynski had dropped a centre, hesitated and saw the ball hacked away from his feet.

City were certainly playing with more conviction and purpose in attack but they found it difficult to create chances and Widzew more than happy with the stalemate pulled men back at the slightest sign of trouble.

1978-79 UEFA CUP

FC TWENTE ENSCHEDE 1   MANCHESTER CITY 1

Goal Scorer: Watson
UEFA Cup
First Round – First Leg, Wednesday 13 September 1978
Diekmanstadion, Holland
Attendance: 12,000

City Team: Corrigan, Clements, Power, Viljoen, Watson, P. Futcher, Channon, Owen, Palmer, Hartford, Barnes
Subs: Macrae (GK), Booth, Bell, Keegan, Henry

PRESS VIEW

City could be criticised for letting Twente off the hook after a first half in which they could have been three up at the break. Roger Palmer missed a couple of fine openings created by the hard working Mike Channon, although the young strikers header that clipped the cross bar on 31 minutes was a gem of an effort. (**Manchester Evening News**)

Gradually City began to climb on top and Watson struck in the 24th minute to punish Twente for the slack marking and to score his first goal in European competition. He leapt to a brilliantly accurate 40 yard free kick from Asa Hartford to glide the ball well beyond the keepers reach. (**Daily Express**)

Corrigan as consistent as ever produced three notable saves in quick succession, but the England keeper could not prevent Twente from equalising in the 51st minute, Thoresen brought down by Watson on the edge box took the free kick himself and the shot was deflected on its way through the wall. (**Daily Telegraph**)

The result might well have gone against City and it might have been a crushing one but for the ever dependable Joe Corrigan. (**Daily Mail**)

I expected more of them particularly in the first half. They did come into the match as a force after half time. (**Brian Kidd**)

We have seen the best of Twente tonight but they have not seen the best of us yet. (**Dave Watson**)

Blues can do it this time

Manchester City are halfway towards laying their UEFA Cup bogey, at the fourth time of asking. A glorious first half of attacking football against the Dutchmen of Twente Enschede followed by a second period of passive resistance leaves the Blues on the brink of surviving the opening round for the first time in four attempts. But for a string of missed first half chances they would already be over the hill and coasting to round two.

However a highly creditable 1-1 draw in the Diekman stadium leaves City firmly in the driving seat for the second leg at Maine Road, when a scoreless draw would be enough to squeeze them through on the strength of the away goals ruling. Yet on the evidence of last night's solid all round show, City should progress in convincing manner by tanning the hides off a side who showed little real courage or conviction until five minutes into the second half

Dave Watson who was a tower of strength throughout was City's hero of the night with his first ever European goal, apart from his goal when stealing forward on a blind side run to find space and head in Asa Hartford's free kick he drove his men relentlessly, especially in the second half when the action was thick and fast in the City penalty area.

MANCHESTER CITY 3   FC TWENTE ENSCHEDE 2

Goal Scorer: Kidd, Bell, Wildschut (OG)

UEFA Cup

First Round – Second Leg, Wednesday 27 September 1978
Maine Road, Manchester
Attendance: 29,330

City Team: Corrigan, Clements, Power, Viljoen (Bell), Watson, P. Futcher, Channon, Owen, Kidd, Hartford, Barnes
Subs: Macrae (GK), Booth, Keegan, Palmer

CITY QUOTES

Tonight's tie while balanced slightly in our favour still has to be won. **(Tony Book)**

I'm looking forward to the game; I am not promising to hit the target, as long as we win through that will do me. **(Brian Kidd)**

We are going for goals to kill them off quickly. **(Tony Book)**

PRESS VIEW

City got the early goal they needed when Gary Owen sprinted wide of the Dutch defence and crossed the ball wickedly that Piet Wildschut turned it into his own goal. (*Daily Mirror*)

Had Twente been blessed with a finishing punch and enjoyed the same sort of chances that came the home side's way, then City might well have been drawing the curtains on Europe there and then. (*Manchester Evening News*)

A free kick 25 yards out seemed to offer little in the way of threat, but the Manchester wall was slow in organising itself. Overwegs realised what was happening and Corrigan getting only a late glimpse of the ball managed only to get a hand to it as it crossed the line. (*The Times*)

More City cheers came when Bell rammed home a 15 yard volley but the Dutchmen, showing plenty of constructive ideas, had something left, Thoresen got past two defenders in a fine burst for Gritter to score at close range. (*Daily Telegraph*)

Bell switch swings UEFA tie for Book's shaky heroes

Manchester City are no longer the frightened and frustrated flops of Europe. However they still managed to scare the pants off their fans before finally laying the UEFA Cup bogey in a Maine Road cliff hanger that remained precariously in the balance until the welcome final whistle.

City were given an unexpected start from a Piet Wildschut own goal after only eight minutes but then lived dangerously from that point wasting at least two first half chances that could have wrapped up the tie there and then and from the moment Niels Overweg rapped in a free kick, the Blues were walking a tightrope of uncertainty as the tie reached a dramatic and entertaining climax.

Brian Kidd and Colin Bell scored the goals that gave City what looked like to be a watertight lead, but even then the Blues diced with death and allowed Twente to pull one back, had the Dutch scored again City would have gone out on the away goals ruling. They did not although there were a few nervous wrecks after a furious final five minutes in which Twente threw everything forward in a last brave and desperate attempt to salvage a great cup tie.

MANCHESTER CITY 4 STANDARD LIEGE 0

Goal Scorer: Kidd (2, 1p) Palmer, Hartford
UEFA Cup
Second Round – First Leg, Wednesday 18 October 1978
Maine Road, Manchester
Attendance: 27,487

City Team: Corrigan, Clements, Donachie, Booth, Watson, Viljoen (Keegan), Palmer, Bell, Kidd, Hartford, Barnes
Subs: Macrae (GK), Futcher, Power, Henry

PRESS VIEW

Maine Roads impatient boo boys came under fire last night, after a sensational grandstand finish earned City a 4-0 win over Standard Liege. Three goals in the last five minutes provided the perfect last gasp answer to the booing section of the crowd, who ended up giving them a standing ovation. (*Daily Mirror*)

Peter Barnes left his magic late as Manchester City hit three goals in the last five minutes to book their passage towards the third round of the UEFA Cup. (*Daily Mail*)

Brilliant Barnes sets up City's siege of Liege

Three crushing goals in the last five minutes at Maine Road enabled Manchester City, a team of contrasting moods, to take an emphatic first leg lead against Standard Liege, experienced European campaigners, in last night's UEFA Cup tie.

City who had their share of anxious moments in a fiercely contested match, made the most of their opportunities in a furious final fling and now look almost certain to reach the third round. For a long time though it looked as if City would have to travel with only Asa Hartford's early goal but the Standard defence caved in disastrously as the brilliant Peter Barnes, turned on all his formidable power. Barnes who had provided the right wing centre from which Hartford scored with a 12th minute header was then involved in all three late occasions, as Brian Kidd with goals in the 86th and 87th minute and Roger Palmer with the final thrust a minute from time sent the crowd home in a jubilant mood.

CITY QUOTES

It was a bit disappointing not getting the right kind of support at a time when you are entitled to expect it. I thought the fans might have realised the importance of being patient on this kind of occasion. (**Asa Hartford**)

These young fans must learn it is not possible to go forward all the time without chancing being caught on the break. It could easily have been 1-1 which would have given us a whole lot to do over in Belgium. Now the only way we can go out is by being stupid. **(Tony Book)**

We are a competent and good enough team to win this tie, we have the strength. (**Joe Mercer**)

STANDARD LIEGE 2   MANCHESTER CITY 0
UEFA Cup
Second Round – Second Leg, Wednesday 1 November 1978
Attendance: 25,000

City Team:
Corrigan, Clements, Donachie, Booth, Watson, Owen, Channon, Bell, Kidd, Hartford, Palmer

PRESS VIEW
There was an explosive ending to what should have been a walk over for City. They went to Belgium leading 4-0, yet lost 2-0 and also had Gary Owen sent off, four minutes from time for retaliation. (*Daily Mail*)

Gary Owen, City's young England captain was sent off after a foolish show of temper four minutes from the end of this UEFA cup tie. A skirmish developed and Owen was rightly shown the red card. (*Daily Mirror*)

Gary Owens short fuse temperament blew again last night to blot an assured and otherwise cool City performance in the UEFA Cup. The young England skipper was sent off for aiming a flying kick at an opponent. (*Daily Express*)

Gary Owen the young England midfield player un-necessarily spoiled the effects of a workman like performance by City by being sent off. (*Guardian*)

No one can possibly make any excuses. Gary had spoilt but not overshadowed one of the finest achievements in the clubs history. (**Peter Swales**)

Gary is in the learning process and there are some painful lessons. I was annoyed in the sense that he went in among their players. He was trying to defend a situation and got a bit caught up in it. (**Tony Book**)

I'm upset but I'm more upset for the team and for my family. I feel I have let them down. It is the first time I have been sent off. All I intended to do was to go in and help Asa. There were about six of them around him after he was fouled and I just felt I had to give him a hand. (**Gary Owen**)

Owen KO sours City's sweet performance

Manchester City were poised gloriously to graduate with European honours until Gary Owen failed the test of temperament. His 86th minute sending off in Belgium was the one souring note of a magnificent Blues performance as they marched defiantly into the last 16 of the UEFA Cup.

Despite last night's 2-0 defeat at the hands of Standard Liege, City go into tomorrow's third round draw on the strength of a 4-2 aggregate success following two gripping ties. However Owen's hot temper means he must temporarily shelve personal European ambitions as UEFA's strict disciplinary authorities are certain to hand out a three match ban to the fiery young England captain who foolishly chased fully 15 yards to aim a flying kick at Phillipe Garot who had just fouled Asa Hartford on the half way line.

AC MILAN 2   MANCHESTER CITY 2

Goal Scorers: Power, Kidd
UEFA Cup
Third Round – First Leg, Thursday 23 November 1978
San Siro Stadium, Milan
Attendance: 40,000

City Team: Corrigan, Clements, Donachie, Booth, Watson, Power, Viljoen (Keegan), Bell, Kidd, Hartford, Palmer
Subs: Macrae (GK), Futcher, Henry, Coughlin

The Italian fans were in full voice anticipating the slaughter of the innocents. Mighty AC Milan were about to deal with Manchester City's challenge in the first leg of the UEFA Cup third round tie.

Firecrackers, smoke bombs and frustrated trumpeters endorsed an atmosphere of intimidation. Injury hit City were without two stars in Mike Channon and Peter Barnes. No British club had emerged from the San Siro Stadium in victory. The result appeared a formality.

As kick off approached thick swirling fog enveloped the stadium and the crowds were silenced by the referee's decision to postpone the match until the next day. The next day the crowd, less volatile and fewer in numbers were silenced again, this time by a Paul Power stunning execution. Early in the second half Power controlled the ball in his own half, raced 65–70 yards into the heart of the Italian defence and clipped a left foot shot past keeper Albertosi. It gave City a 2-0 lead and one of the finest hours in Europe was only dimmed by the Italians late equaliser.

PRESS VIEW

Powerful Italian pressure at the beginning of the second half was promptly answered by a second City goal in the 57th minute. Watson broke up a Milan raid and Power showed tremendous pace when running 70 yards to the other penalty area and holding off two challengers before hitting a low left footed shot under the diving keeper. (***Daily Telegraph***)

Three times Milan had goals disallowed for offside as the City defence withstood tremendous pressure when the home side fought back from two down to draw. Central defenders Tommy Booth and Dave Watson were masters of the air and the midfield coped superbly with Rivera and Buriani. (***Daily Express***)

With eight minutes left City led 2-1 and the Milan supporters were already leaving, pausing only to hurl seat cushions and abuse their players. Then an intricate attack ended with Albertino Bigon breaking clear of the outstanding Dave Watson and Booth to equalise from close range for his second goal of the match. (***Daily Star***)

Italian fans, as only they can, still caused a riot because of their own team's shortcomings and tear gas bombs were thrown to disperse the crowds. (***Manchester Evening News***)

Milan halved the lead two minutes after City scored when Bigon forced the ball over the line from Walter Novellinos cross and immediately City faced increasing pressure. Three times Corrigan was beaten, but each time the linesman flag was raised for offside. The decisions disgusted the crowd, some of who took out their spite on Corrigan by pelting him with rubbish. (***Daily Mirror***)

Manchester City have come of age as a major European force to be feared. Any side that steps into the passion of the hostile San Siro stadium and comes within seven agonising minutes of victory has got to be reckoned with. Their performance in holding AC Milan to 2-2 was one of the greatest efforts by a British team on the continent in years. (***Manchester Evening News***)

Admittedly, City had a let off after only one minute when, rounding off a brilliant move triggered off by the cunning Rivera, full back Fulvio Collovati shot wide with the goal at his mercy. Yet far from losing their composure over this threat City swung the ball with great flair and taking their own time about it virtually played the crafty Italians at their own game. (***Daily Mail***)

For a quarter of an hour Rivera used the freedom City had afforded him in midfield to give a passing exhibition which kept the Mancunian defence busy, but fortunately Booth and Watson were in commanding form. As they grew in confidence City began to look the more likely to score, although they could hardly have expected it to be as easy as when Hartford's orthodox deep cross drifted over from the left and Kidd headed calmly across Albertosi into the net. (***Guardian***)

PLAYER & MANAGEMENT QUOTES

I thought Milan's equalising goal was at least two yards offside, but I am extremely delighted and extremely satisfied with the result. (**Tony Book**)

I can't think of a better performance in the four and half years I have been manager of this club. It was a truly magnificent effort by everyone. (**Tony Book**)

We had the audacity to go two goals up at the San Siro. It was a tough ground to play at, fireworks going off and an intimidating atmosphere. No one ever beat them at home but we were. They came back at us and it ended 2-2. (**Kenny Clements**)

The game against AC Milan should have been played on the Wednesday evening. We got to the San Siro Stadium and got stripped, but a fog descended like you would not believe. They kept us there for an hour, hoping to start the game but it was impossible. So the match was scheduled for the Thursday afternoon. Many of the local supporters were at work, so with the stadium not full the atmosphere was not as intense as it would have been the previous evening which suited us. We went two goals up and though Milan pulled the match level it was a great result and a tremendous performance. (**Paul Power**)

SUPPORTER'S VIEW

One of the most bizarre games I have witnessed in all the time I have been watching City was an away tie against AC Milan.

As one of a party of four, I flew early on the Wednesday morning for the game, which was due to kick off at eight o'clock that evening. It was bright sunshine that greeted us at Milan airport and from there we were taken to our hotel. A quick change soon saw us in one of the many local bars and we soon grasped the language 'Quattro Beero, please'.

At around four o'clock, one of the locals entered the bar and approached us 'you boys over for the game' he asked, 'yes' we replied in unison, 'game off' he said, 'what you talking about?' we replied. He went on 'fog, fog come down from the mountains, game off'. Quick as a flash we all rushed to the nearest window. The sun was still shining and we could literally see for miles. 'Oh, yes very funny' we said, the local was adamant 'no, no its off, fog'.

At about 6.30 p.m. the coach arrived to take us to the ground. Within an hour, the fog made its appearance. We were dropped off about thirty yards from the ground and we could not see a single brick of the massive San Siro Stadium. We eventually made our way in and all we could see were hazy images of the many fires started on the terracing to keep the Milan fans warm, any hint of green grass was completely out of the question. There were many announcements over a high quality public address system, the only thing was not one of them was in English.

After what seemed an eternity, we were finally told that there was no chance of play that night. We were then told to go to the ticket office where we could get replacement tickets for the re-arranged fixture the following day at 12 noon.

Because our return flight was at two o'clock, we could either miss the second half or miss our flight. At half time with City winning 2-0 we decided the game was ours and it was safe to get the flight back. A Milan supporter who had a television over his rear view mirror and spent the entire trip watching the second half drove the coach back to the airport.

We nearly missed everything when Milan pulled a goal back. The driver leapt from his seat and began jumping around in the aisle before being persuaded to sit back down. Just before we boarded the plane Milan equalised and the game finished 2-2. **(Daniel Thomas)**

MANCHESTER CITY 3   AC MILAN 0

Goal Scorers: Kidd, Booth, Hartford
UEFA Cup
Third Round – Second Leg, Wednesday 6 December 1978
Maine Road, Manchester
Attendance: 38,026

City Team: Corrigan, Keegan, Donachie, Booth, Watson, Power, Channon, Viljoen, Kidd, Hartford, Barnes
Subs: Macrae (GK), Futcher, Palmer

PRE-MATCH QUOTES

It will be a cat and mouse tie tonight. They will I am sure have the typical Italian approach in these classic cases where one goal has to be snatched to turn defeat into victory. We have a squad of players who are capable of going right through to the final. **(Tony Book)**

Whoever wins must be regarded as probable finalists. That's how important this game is. **(Niels Liedholm, Milan's Swedish coach)**

PRESS VIEW

Majestic Manchester City emerged as the first true English masters of once mighty Milan last night as an ecstatic crowd celebrated a 3-0 victory. (*Daily Mirror*)

It was City's most impressive victory in Europe and Italy's national team manager Enzo Bearzot described it as a magnificent performance. (*Daily Mail*)

MANCHESTER CITY 1   BORUSSIA MONCHENGLADBACH 1

Goal Scorer: Channon
UEFA Cup
Fourth Round – First Leg, Wednesday 7 March 1979
Maine Road, Manchester
Attendance: 39,005

City Team: Corrigan, Donachie, Power, Reid, Watson, Booth, Channon, Viljoen, Kidd, Hartford, Barnes

PRESS VIEW

Manchester City took another turn for the worse at Maine Road last night. Their prospects of reaching the semi-final of the UEFA cup, the only competition that they still have an interest in, can be considered little more than marginal, as Gladbach returned to West Germany with the insurance of an away goal. (*Guardian*)

A fleeting moment of magic by the man, whom Kevin Keegan regards as the best footballer in the world, cut Manchester City's chance of survival in Europe. It came in the 67th minute of an exciting first leg at Maine Road when Allan Simonsen diverted the ball from team mate Ewald Liener to equalise. (*Daily Mail*)

City's theme song, which includes the line 'The Boys will never give in', thundered over Maine Road as usual, but few believed it after Borussia had held on and then threatened to humble a team whose season continues to go wildly wrong. (*Daily Mirror*)

Germans rally takes gloss of City display

A smart early goal by the transfer listed Mike Channon was all Manchester City could manage from countless all-out attacks in last night's UEFA Cup quarter-final at Maine Road, and Monchengladbach got the first leg result they wanted with a second half equaliser from Erwald Lienen.

City who played sparkling football at times without producing the finishing power needed against top class European opposition, now face a demanding task in Germany if they are to reach the semi finals.

Tempers flared on occasions and Alex Ponnet the Belgian referee produced the yellow card when booking two players on each side for fouls and there was tension on the touchline when Borussia held up play by delaying the introduction of their substitutes and Malcolm Allison, City's coach exchanged angry words with his opposite number Udo Lattek.

City's goal came after 24 minutes. Hartford's shot bounced off Barnes and before a defender could move to intercept, Channon raced in to hit a low right footed shot into the far corner. With most of the spectators roaring them on. City looked for further goals. Hartford, Booth and Kidd were all near but the Germans proved dangerous on the break and the 'away' goal City could not afford to concede came in the 67th minute after a couple of near misses. Simonsen played the ball through for Lienen to take his time and place a close range shot past Corrigan's right hand.

MANAGEMENT VIEW

Don't count us out, we can still do it. We go to Germany with high hopes. We could have scored three or four goals tonight with better finishing Borussia are no better than the three teams we have already knocked out so far. (**Tony Book**)

We expect to face a different City in the second leg. An away goal is priceless but we have to start all over again. (**Udo Lattek**)

BORUSSIA MONCHENGLADBACH 3   MANCHESTER CITY 1

Goal Scorer: Deyna
UEFA Cup
Fourth Round – Second Leg, Tuesday 20 March 1979
Boelkelberg Stadium, Germany
Attendance: 30,000

City Team: Corrigan, Donachie, Power, Viljoen, Watson, Booth, Channon, Reid (Deyna), Henry, Hartford, Barnes

PRESS VIEW

Manchester City are wondering what they can salvage from the remainder of their abysmal season after being out witted by Borussia in the second leg of the quarter final of the UEFA Cup. (*Guardian*)

Manchester City slipped out of Europe when they failed to match the counter punching power of the West Germans, failing to produce the pace or finishing power to capitalise on the fine midfield work by Colin Viljoen and Asa Hartford. (*Daily Mail*)

Manchester City's last, lingering hope of salvaging something from a disastrous season was extinguished with emphatic defeat in the UEFA Cup. They were impressive enough in the opening half hour but the task imposing already was always beyond them once Borussia scored on either side of half time. (*Daily Mirror*)

Manchester City's brave European dream is now nothing more than a nightmare memory. (*Manchester Evening News*)

> ### SHATTERED-Great Danes shoot down City
> The power and guile of Borussia sent City crashing out of the UEFA Cup last night and City were left to reflect on the missed chances in the first leg in the 1-1 draw at Maine Road.
>
> City could have taken the lead just before half time when new boy Tony Henry bent a 20-yarder crashing into a Borussia upright, but with City's defence exposed Borussia swept away and Christian Kulik had an easy chance to put his side one up. Borussia, the side that thrives on striking quickly from defence broke out with another lighting raid in the 51st minute, Del Haye swooping on City's goal and crossed for Allan Simonsen to reach and Bruns darted in to make it 2-0. Del Haye himself moved with menacing speed in the 72nd minute to snap up another chance.
>
> City's revival coincided with the appearance of Kaziu Deyna and it was Deyna who scored City's goal in the 78th minute when he sweetly volleyed in a cross from Mike Channon.

PLAYER & MANAGEMENT QUOTES

The Germans can be exploited at dead ball situations and we have got to hammer this advantage. We have an immense advantage in the air, if we rush forward with free kicks and corners there is a chance we can catch the Germans napping. (**Tony Book**)

Our tactics were right but it did not work out for us on the night. It all hinged on their goal just before half time after we had hit the post. We had the better chances in the first half while in the second we had push up to stop them getting possession at the back. (**Malcolm Allison**)

There were two aspects at which they were outstanding. Their finishing was clinical and the disciplined man for man marking is something which the Germans are good at. (**Tony Book**)

The big problem was the return of Malcolm Allison. I knew he was a great coach first time round at City, but second time he really did ruin everything. All the older players told me it would be great having him back, and then when he was back they admitted they were all wrong. I think he became too hung up new ideas that he forgot about the basics. (**Kenny Clements**)

City's approach to the game mystified the Germans.
I was surprised right from the start that City did not attack us as much as we thought they would. A goalless draw was sufficient for us but City did not have any alternative but to score goals. We found it hard to understand why they were not pushing men forward in attack. They seemed to spend the whole game concentrating on midfield.
(Allan Simonsen, skipper of Borussia)

PLAYER Q&A

ASA HARTFORD

Manchester City playing record
1974–1979
1981–1984
321 Games
36 Goals

What is your most vivid memory of playing in Europe?
Being knocked out by Borussia.

Did you prefer the home legs or the away legs, and why?
I did not have any preference.

Who was the most difficult opponent you faced?
Marco Tardelli of Juventus.

Whose was the most passionate support you played in front of?
A friendly at Club Bruges. I was 17 and playing in Europe for the first time.

Did any fellow City players have a fear of flying, hate foreign food or was a real grouch at dealing with foreigners?
Not to my knowledge, although equally that does not mean that we all loved flying.

Was playing in Europe more important than the domestic game?
It was not more important but it was more exciting.

How did you feel once the City side you were playing for was knocked out of Europe?
Deflated as though it was unnecessary. Malcolm Allison played two young inexperienced players instead of Kazi Deyna and Brian Kidd.

If there was one thing you could change about your European adventures with City, what would it be?
Malcolm Allison would not have played the side that he did in Germany.

KENNY CLEMENTS

Manchester City playing record
1971–1979
1985–1987
282 Games
2 Goals

What is your most vivid memory of playing in Europe?
The 2-2 draw at AC Milan, we went 2-0 up and held onto a 2-2 draw in the end. We won 3-1 at Maine Road and I got man of the match playing centre half as Dave Watson was injured.

Did you prefer the home legs or the away legs, and why?
Home or Away, it never seemed to bother me. I enjoyed the experience of new stadiums and did not suffer with nerves at all.

Who was the most difficult opponent you faced?
I cannot remember any special names, so they cannot have been that difficult.

What was the funniest incident you can remember, or will admit to?
When Paul Power lost a contact lens and then proceeded to look for it.

What was the food like abroad?
Never a problem, chips taste the same everywhere.

Whose was the most passionate support you played in front of?
The Kippax.

Did any fellow City players have a fear of flying, hate foreign food or was a real grouch at dealing with foreigners?
Mike Doyle, Asa Hartford & Peter Barnes did not like flying; we made it worse by cracking Glen Miller & Buddy Holly jokes.

Was playing in Europe more important than the domestic game?
Not more important, but a welcome break from it.

If there was one thing you could change about your European adventures with City, what would it be?
Keep the excellent team we had in Tony Book and the late Bill Taylor.

TOMMY BOOTH

Manchester City playing record
1968–1981
491 Games
37 Goals

What is your most vivid memory of playing in Europe?
Winning the European Cup Winners' Cup in Vienna against Gornik.

Did you prefer the home legs or the away legs, and why?
I preferred to play the away leg first knowing you knew what was required in the home leg.

Who was the most difficult opponent you faced?
Johan Cruyff.

What was the funniest incident you can remember, or will admit to?
One of the lads entertaining a lady after a match. Turned out to be a fella.

What was the food like abroad?
In most countries the food was good, the exception was Poland.

Whose was the most passionate support you played in front of?
Barcelona & Real Madrid.

Did any fellow City players have a fear of flying, hate foreign food or was a real grouch at dealing with foreigners?
Arthur Mann, he had a fear of flying.

Was playing in Europe more important than the domestic game?
You had to do well in the League to qualify for Europe; they both complimented one and other.

How did you feel once the City side you were playing for was knocked out of Europe?
It was a bitter blow to everyone at the club, but at least you still had the domestic competitions to play for.

If there was one thing you could change about your European adventures with City, what would it be?
To play in the Champions League today.

TONY HENRY

Manchester City playing record
1975–1981
93 Games
12 Goals

What is your most vivid memory of playing in Europe?
Playing against Borussia in Germany. We lost 3-1 and I hit the bar from thirty yards at 0-0.

Did you prefer the home legs or the away legs. And why?
Both games had a tremendous atmosphere; the away tie was always a lot harder.

Who was the most difficult opponent you faced?
Buetragueno.

What was the funniest incident you can remember, or will admit to?
I tripped up on the trackside as I came on against AC Milan.

What was the food like abroad?
I eat anything. I lived in Japan for two years and loved the raw fish.

Whose was the most passionate support you played in front of?
AC Milan.

Did any fellow City players have a fear of flying, hate foreign food or was a real grouch at dealing with foreigners?
Asa Hartford hated flying, Kenny Clements was a fish and chip man but normally we did not upset the foreigners especially in their own backyard.

Was playing in Europe more important than the domestic game?
Playing in Europe was just a bonus for all the hard work you had put in.

How did you feel once the City side you were playing for was knocked out of Europe?
All players hate losing games. It makes it worse if you have a 3-4 hour flight home.

If there was one thing you could change about your European adventures with City, what would it be?
I would not change a thing. It was a fantastic experience and something I feel very privileged and lucky to be have involved with.

WILLIE DONACHIE

Manchester City playing record
1969–1979
436 Games
2 Goals

What is your most vivid memory of playing in Europe?
The first game in the quarter final of the Cup Winners' Cup against Gornik of Poland, we were 2-0 down, we won the next game 2-0 and then won the play off.

Did you prefer the home legs or the away legs, and why?
The home games because of the atmosphere of the game and the support of the fans.

Who was the most difficult opponent you faced?
Causioi of Juventus.

What was the funniest incident you can remember, or will admit to?
Mike Lester came on as sub against Juventus and Gentile immediately charged him and almost knocked him out.

What was the food like abroad?
Mainly rubbish.

Whose was the most passionate support you played in front of?
Juventus.

Did any fellow City players have a fear of flying, hate foreign food or was a real grouch at dealing with foreigners?
Arthur Mann, he had a fear of flying.

Was playing in Europe more important than the domestic game?
No.

How did you feel once the City side you were playing for was knocked out of Europe?
Very disappointed.

If there was one thing you could change about your European adventures with City, what would it be?
Enjoy it more.

2003-04 UEFA CUP

MANCHESTER CITY 5   TOTAL NETWORK SOLUTIONS (TNS) 0

Goal Scorers: Sommeil, Anelka, Sinclair, Wright-Phillips, Jihai Sun

UEFA Cup
Qualifying Round – First Leg, Thursday 14 August 2003
City of Manchester Stadium

Attendance: 34,103

This was City's first European game since 1978–79 and it was also the opening competitive fixture at their new stadium.

City Team: Seaman, Sommeil, Distin, Berkovic, Jihai Sun, Tarnat (Tiatto), Bosvelt, (Barton) Wright-Phillips, Sinclair,
Subs: Weaver (GK), Huckerby, Wiekens, Dunne

MANAGEMENT QUOTES

This is our fifth season in Europe so we are more experienced than City when it comes to European football. This is the best news in TNS's history. I feel sorry for City; they wait 24 years to get back into Europe only for it to end in defeat in Wrexham. (**A joking TNS managing director, Mike Harris**)

Our fans have waited a long time for this and we promised then we would get back to this level eventually. (**John Wardle**)

I would rather have qualified for Europe the conventional way by winning a Cup or finishing in the top six of the league but for us it could be a case of in the back door and out of the front. (**Kevin Keegan**)

We have approached our games with TNS very professionally and prepared properly. We have had them watched four times and left no stone unturned. It is quite easy to say they are a small club, that they do not play in a strong league and all those kinds of things, but when you actually see them, they are well organised and know what they are trying to do. We have to treat them with total respect and that is what we have done. (**Kevin Keegan**)

Five was probably a fair reflection of the game but some of the goals we conceded were disappointing with a couple down to goalkeeping errors, but at this level if you make a mistake you get punished. Hopefully we will learn our lessons from this. (**Ken McKenna, TNS manager**)

PRESS VIEW

Facing poor opposition on a perfect surface in the balmy warmth of August can make football an easy business, but in beating part time opposition from Wales, Manchester City showed enough to suggest they may be able to match the lofty ambitions of their manager Kevin Keegan. (*Daily Mail*)

The village side should be proud of a gritty first half performance, during which they restricted their illustrious opponents to a single goal. They may have heaped more embarrassment had it not been for a few unfortunate errors by the keeper Ged Doherty, who seemingly allowed his nerves to get the better of him. (*Liverpool Daily Post*)

Doubtless, TNS and the clutch of boisterous sight seers who had followed them from Wales harboured aspirations of inflicting painful humiliation on a club who had waited 24 years since their last venture into Europe. (*Guardian*)

The part timers of TNS were by no means disgraced as they frustrated Manchester City for much of this UEFA Cup qualifier. (*Daily Telegraph*)

In the end the vast gulf showed with the Premiership class of the City slickers proving too much for the stubborn tenacity of TNS. The mid Wales team battled with heart, keeping their shape and discipline to repel some unrelenting pressure and incisive moment from a star studded City side. (*Shropshire Star*)

Not even Manchester City with their renowned penchant for self-destruction could poop their own house warming party, but it took some time before they were allowed to feel at home in their new surroundings. (*The Times*)

TOTAL NETWORK SOLUTIONS (TNS)   0 MANCHESTER CITY 2

Goal Scorers: Negouai, Huckerby
UEFA Cup
Qualifying Round – Second Leg, Thursday 28 August 2003
Millennium Stadium, Cardiff
Attendance: 10,123

City Team: Weaver, Flood, Dunne, Wiekens, Bischoff, Tiatto, Bosvelt (Whelan), Negouai, Berkovic (Barton), Huckerby, Macken (Wright-Phillips
Subs: Ellegaard (GK), Distin, Sinclair, Jihai Sun

With the Recreation Field at Llansantffraid only holding around 2,000 people, Welsh village side TNS confirmed they will play their home UEFA Cup tie against Manchester City at the Millennium Stadium.

There had been some debate over the choice of venue

for the second leg on 28 August, with Wrexham's Racecourse Ground in the running until it was discovered the Welsh rugby team were due to play there against Romania the previous evening.

PRESS VIEW

Unlucky fans accompanying Manchester City on their first European away day for 25 years had to put up with rain, the tortuous M6, M50 roadwork's, Cardiff congestion and even the Monmouth show, but their day did not really turn sour until the match started.

No matter what disruption they encountered on their way to the Millennium stadium, nothing could have been as dismal as the fare their team served up against TNS. They got the win their manager demanded and advanced into the first round proper of the UEFA Cup. **(Press Association)**

City made ten changes from the first leg, deciding to rest a host of first team players with the tie all-but over. (*Sporting Life*)

TNS played with far more confidence than in Manchester, and could easily have taken a first half lead. Chris Taylor wasted a golden chance to open the scoring when he could only head weakly wide after Nicky Weaver had flapped at a cross. **(Welsh Premier League)**

I think we were worth a draw, our performance justified our decision to bring the match to Cardiff and although we were well beaten overall, I feel very proud of how the players have performed. **(Ken McKenna TNS)**

MANCHESTER CITY 3   SPORTING LOKEREN OV 2

Goal Scorers: Anelka (P), Fowler, Sibierski
UEFA Cup
First Round – First Leg, Wednesday 24 September 2003
City of Manchester Stadium
Attendance: 29,067

City Team: Seaman, Tiatto (Dunne), Distin, Sommeil, Jihai Sun, Sibierski, McManaman, Reyna, Bosvelt (Wright-Phillips), Anelka, Fowler (Sinclair)
Subs: Weaver (GK), Barton, Berkovic, Jordan

PRESS VIEW

Although City recovered from 2-1 down to secure a narrow lead, Lokeren's two away goals will make the return a potentially treacherous occasion in Eastern Flanders. (*Guardian*)
Manchester City came from behind to secure a slender

advantage for the second leg of their Uefa Cup first-round tie against Belgian side Lokeren.

Kevin Keegan's side looked to be heading for a shock defeat at the City of Manchester Stadium despite dominating for long periods. **(BBC)**

They took the lead when Sibierski curled home his 20-yard effort after Anelka had been fouled.

Yet, from their position of total dominance, City had the rug pulled from under their feet and Seaman, whose error count has been growing in recent weeks, was again at fault. But salvation was on hand as Fowler toed City level before Jihai was sent flying inside the penalty area, giving Anelka the chance to seal victory with his seventh goal of a productive campaign. *(Sporting Life)*

MANAGEMENT QUOTE

We needed the crowd to get behind us but they booed us off in our own stadium. I find that terribly disappointing, they were starting to get to one or two players. It is not what you need when things are not going your way.

I have never had a team which has been booed off before. If players are not trying I won't protect them but they were working really hard and didn't deserve that treatment. **(Kevin Keegan)**

SPORTING LOKEREN OV 0   MANCHESTER CITY 1

Goal Scorer: Anelka (P)
UEFA Cup
First Round – Second Leg, Wednesday 15 October 2003
Daknam Stadium
Attendance: 10,000

City Team:
Seaman, Jihai Sun, Sommeil, Distin, Tarnat, Wright-Phillips, Sinclair (Barton), McManaman, Bosvelt, Wanchope (Reyna), Anelka
Subs: Weaver (GK), Wiekens, Berkovic, Sibierski, Fowler

PRESS VIEW

Anelka made sure Manchester City came through a potentially embarrassing night in Belgium with pride intact. The French striker scored a 19th minute penalty to give Kevin Keegan's side a 4-2 aggregate success.

Lokeren fans were in high spirits at the start despite their team having failed to win in 17 league outings since the spring, a sequence which has left them at the foot of the Belgian League. *(Daily Telegraph)*

The dream of European glory goes on for Manchester City after Nicolas Anelka scored his eighth goal of the season. City back in Europe for the first time in 25 years brought 4,000 supporters with them and they made up half the crowd in this neat little ground and those supporters were getting restless and desperate for a second goal to put the game out of Lokeren's reach but fortunately the home side ran out of steam. **(Press Association)**

Those 4,000 supporters initially had severe travel instructions placed upon them and several independent companies were advertising trips.

Manchester City as a club also published their own set of travel details.

Eventually as the day of the match approached the Belgian side and police announced a relaxation in ticket arrangements, with travelling fans now welcome in the town of Lokeren and fans being allowed to travel independently to the area

Kevin's Boys Nic Glory

Nicolas Anelka last night ensured there was no embarrassing early end to Manchester City's first European Campaign for 24 years. As the £13m striker kept his nerve to score a 17th minute penalty there was enough to steer Kevin Keegan's team into the UEFA Cup second round on a 4-2 aggregate.

With only a narrow 3-2 win from the first leg, this was a potential banana skin for unpredictable City, especially with their confidence dented by their shock defeat at Wolves in their last Premiership outing. But Anelka's early strike eased any anxieties and they produced a disciplined performance against the team who are propping up Belgium's first division and who have gone 17 league games without a win.

City moved into a two goal aggregate lead when Paulo Wanchope went down in the penalty area while marshalled by Mamadou Coulibaly. Anelka kept his cool and scored his eighth goal of the season.

Yes, slick Nic did the business and City's Euro dream continues.

SUPPORTERS' VIEWS

'Really enjoyed it. First European away trip for me. Seemed like we completely invaded the place. More city fans in the ground than them. And I used to love the chant where we all swung our scarves around.'

'The security at the game was a joke, ticketless Blues getting in by flashing beer mats at the stewards.'

'Great trip but I'm still amazed that stand did not collapse with all the freeloaders as well as the 4,000 'official' blues jumping up and down.'

MANAGEMENT VIEW

We have done what we had to do in Lokeren, but it was a tough game, I think we were fortunate to get the penalty in the first half. The surface for both sides was very difficult. If they had converted one of the two chances which they had in the first half then we would have had a very difficult match. They gave us a tough game, we have gone through but it was not easy for us. **(Kevin Keegan)**

PLAYER VIEW

It was not a great spectacle but it was not an easy game. Lokeren competed hard, no one expected them to win and they played without fear. **(Nicolas Anelka)**

We were on a hiding to nothing if we had not performed, these kind of ties are always difficult. **(Steve McManaman)**

SUPPORTERS' TALES

The first round proper brought Lokeren out of the hat and my vast knowledge of European football combined with a distinction in Geography, told me that Lokeren was in Belgium and that was where Stella was made.

There were eight of us travelling in two cars. The drive down was uneventful, the highlight being driving onto the ferry I felt special like Knightrider driving onto his lorry.

We found our hotel ok and we settled in for our 3 night stay just outside of Brussels. Up early we did a bit of sightseeing, Antwerp, Bruges and a wander around Brussels before finding ourselves in a quaint little bar sampling the local brew and the delights of Brussels by night.

We arrived in Lokeren in the early afternoon and set about getting wasted, we partied all afternoon and long into the night, with the match somewhere in the middle.

During the day we bumped into some of our mates who did not have tickets for the match and later found out they tried to gain access to the ground with their train tickets and hey presto they got in. **(CTIC)**

What can be easier than catching a flight from East Midlands Airport to Brussels at 7.30 a.m., well-being stood on the main road of Burnley at 4 a.m., twenty-four hours before I was due to depart, was only the start of my problems.

There then followed a bout of discussion about who said what and when they were going and all the rest of it, but the bottom line was I had missed my flight. Fortunately I managed to get a flight for the following day and I was in Brussels train station early evening, even then the automatic doors close on me at Brussels central and I end up about five miles further down the line.

So a taxi back to the centre and I then spend the next two hours trying to find the Holiday Inn in 'City Centre Brussels', would you believe there are four of them. When

I arrive at reception lo and behold stood there are five lads who sit with me at City. So after a quick freshen up we are on a couple of trams and head for what is reputed the meeting point for most City fans in Brussels that night. The Grand Platz and O'Reillys Irish bar and so the drinks flowed, songs were sung in a real friendly atmosphere and then it was back to the hotel for a couple of late night drinks.

The following morning our transport arrived and we soon set off to Lokeren via Antwerp. We managed to park at the end of the road leading to the ground, just five minutes away and our first indicator we are close to the ground is when six armoured personnel and a water cannon drive past us, as we walk up to the ground we have to pass through a checkpoint, manned by numerous bulky police and a lengthy barbed wire fence. But to be fair the coppers were in good spirits and their unwillingness to closely check tickets has now become legendary as City fans were getting in with train tickets and beer mats.

The game itself was poor and we won with a dodgy penalty which kept the five thousand or so City fans happy and the only real bit of interest was there seemed to be a bit of a jolly punch up going on in one of the stands, we later found out it was rival Belgian fans fighting with each other. **(Tom Ritchie)**

MANCHESTER CITY 1   GROCLIN DYSKOBOLIA 1

Goal Scorer: Anelka
UEFA Cup
Second Round – First Leg, Thursday 6 November 2003
City of Manchester Stadium
Attendance: 32,506

> **City Team:** Seaman, Jihai Sun, Tarnat, Dunne, Distin, Barton, Wright-Phillips, Reyna (Bosvelt), McManaman (Tiatto), Anelka, Fowler (Wanchope)
> Subs: Ellegaard (GK), Sibierski, Macken, Sommeil

PRESS VIEW

Nicolas Anelka was on target once again tonight, but Manchester City have a fight on their hands to remain in the UEFA Cup. The French striker made the breakthrough in the sixth minute. Instead of City growing in confidence, it was the unsung Polish side that started to gain the upper hand. Sebastian Mila grabbed a superb equaliser midway through the second half and they will fancy their chances in the second leg at the end of the month. **(Press Association)**

Kevin Keegan's men must now overcome a potentially treacherous trip to Poland; Groclin will be encouraged by the vulnerabilities that Keegan has failed to eradicate among his players. A fine result for the Polish visitors and just reward for their entertaining supporters who were backed throughout by a superb travelling band. (*Sporting Life*)

Blues fizzle out

Six minutes into this tie Anelka carved Groclin wide open, sashaying between flying Polish boots the final incision had goalkeeper Mariusz Liberda flapping at fresh air. After such a start it was hard to envisage such a disappointing ending to the night for City as the Blues ran out of ideas, momentum and creativity. Groclin were the more energetic of the two sides for the last half hour and thoroughly deserved the treasured away goal that they will have in their locker for the second leg in three weeks' time.

It was really no more than Groclin's enterprise deserved when in the 66th minute Sebastian Mila shot them level with a free kick of stunning power, accuracy and bend and sent the musical band that accompanied the visitors into raptures.

Thereafter the Poles undid some of their goodwill their bright and inventive football had created with a series of dying swan acts that kept the stretcher bearers busy for several minutes but didn't actually necessitate any medical attention.

PLAYER VIEW

We missed a few chances and they kept digging away. A draw was probably a fair result. Our away record has been pretty decent this year and we are confident we will get the result we need. (**Richard Dunne**)

We had a few chances at the start and the end that you would expect us to take and do better. We knew it would be tough and we are very disappointed we did not win. (**Paul Bosvelt**)

MANAGEMENT VIEW

We created some really good chances in the game, especially early on. Finishing those chances off is an art and we did not do that in the game. I think we missed those chances mainly because of our concentration in the second half we could not get ahead of steam. If you are a City supporter you will be disappointed, but so am I and so are the players. (**Kevin Keegan**)

GROCLIN DYSKOBOLIA 0   MANCHESTER CITY 0

UEFA Cup
Second Round – Second Leg, Thursday 27 November 2003
Stadion 'Groclin Dyskobolia'
Attendance: 5,500

City Team: Seaman, Jihai Sun, Dunne, Sommeil, Distin, Barton, Wright-Phillips (Reyna), McManaman. Anelka (Macken), Fowler (Wanchope), Sinclair
Subs: Ellegaard (GK), Wiekens, Bosvelt, Sibierski

PRESS VIEW

Manchester City were sent crashing out of the Uefa Cup after failing to make the breakthrough against a dogged Groclin Dyskobolia in Poland.

In a disjointed performance, City wasted a host of excellent chances, with strikers Nicolas Anelka and Robbie Fowler the most culpable.

Groclin knew a goalless draw would be enough to see them through after grabbing an important away goal in the first leg.

And they got they result they needed, although they had numerous chances to win on their own turf. **(BBC)**

The fog had lifted and the snow never fell as all potential excuses were wiped off City's agenda. With 16 minutes remaining Anelka finally escaped the shackles but his shot was well saved by keeper Mariusz Liberda, it was City's last chance and they were soon out of the UEFA Cup. (*The Times*)

The fireworks lit up the night sky as the little Polish club advanced to the third round of the UEFA cup. Kevin Keegan might feel like launching a few of his own after this shameful display. Anelka and Fowler squandered good chances and it proved costly. City looked short on ideas and invention and there was little spark in the middle of the park. **(Press Association)**

PLAYER & MANAGEMENT QUOTES

We are upset for the fans that spent a lot and travelled a long way. We are bitterly disappointed and we know that the supporters are too. Groclin got the result they wanted, but we can and must do better. **(Shaun Wright-Phillips)**

Groclin are in the third round because they deserve to be. We do not. **(Kevin Keegan)**

SUPPORTER'S VIEW

I like City to play glorious football the whole time and yes patient was the correct way to play at the start but an upping of the tempo was clearly required, after all we did have to score and it was frankly non-existent. The second half was probably slower than the first. Hoofing long balls vaguely in the direction of the penalty box basically never comes off as far as my City watching is concerned, so why do it?

I'm not sure what Keegan's tactics were really: Wright-Phillips are most effective player was substituted. A draw was a fair result; Groclin had one dangerous spell and should have scored (Dunne with an excellent goal line clearance and Fowler off the line from a corner).

City had some decent chances but there was very little clear cut stuff. Anelka had one decent one and should have scored but frankly did not look as though he fancied it today.

A learning experience I hope although part of me doubts it.

2008-09 UEFA CUP

MANCHESTER CITY 0   FC MIDTJYLLAND 1
UEFA Cup
Second Qualifying Round – First Leg, Thursday 14 August 2008
City of Manchester Stadium
Attendance: 17,200

City Team: Hart, Corluka, Richards, Dunne, Ben-Haim, Johnson, Fernandes, Petrov, Elano, (Etuhu), Sturridge, Caicedo (Bojinov)
Subs: Schmeichel (GK), Ball, Onuoha, Ireland, Hamann

PRESS VIEW

Mark Hughes was desperate for City to spark their troubled season by getting off to a flyer. Instead their first competitive match at Eastland's was a flop. Hughes can only hope there is much more to come from his players. If not a troubled pre-season will escalate into chaos. (***Daily Star***)

Mark Hughes week went from bad to worse as City crashed to a shock UEFA Cup defeat. It was the last thing Hughes needed after days of chaos and uncertainty, when his future and that of owner Thaksin Shinawatra has been under a big question mark. (***Daily Mail***)

Fifteen minutes of sloppy passing, running down blind alleys and poor shooting were cruelly punished by the fleet footed Danes. It was a bad night to top off another strange week in the life of Manchester City. (***Manchester Evening News***)

Manchester City suffered a humiliating home defeat by Danish side FC Midtjylland in the first leg of their Uefa Cup second qualifying round tie.

The Danes took the lead on 15 minutes when Danny Olsen punished Richard Dunne's mistake with a precise finish.

City had made a dreadful start but did improve and Daniel Sturridge smashed a shot against the bar before half-time.

Martin Petrov also hit the woodwork with a late free-kick but City could not turn their possession into chances.

Mark Hughes's side will still fancy their chances in the return leg in a fortnight's time but they will need to find a greater cutting edge in Denmark if they are to get the win they need to progress. (***BBC***)

STUPID. Minnow's boss gives Hughes flops a rocket

Manchester City were branded 'stupid' last night as they suffered a grim European humiliation. Mark Hughes side were booed off after being beaten by Danish unknowns FC Midtjylland and afterwards the Danes coach Thomas Tomasberg tore into the Premier League side. He rapped "Maybe they didn't know the names of any single player in our team. Maybe they made stupid decisions, because they lost the ball and thought it would be so easy to get it back".

Midtjylland's goal was swift and clinical but came from a mistake by home captain and centre back Richard Dunne. He was caught in possession by Judah Nworuh before Olsen rammed the ball in across Joe Hart from just inside the area.

FC MIDTJYLLAND 0   MANCHESTER CITY 1

Goal Scorer: Califf (OG)
City won 4-2 on penalties
UEFA Cup
Second Qualifying Round – Second Leg, Thursday 28 August 2008
SAS Arena, Herning, Denmark
Attendance: 9,522

City Team: Hart, Corluka, Ben-Haim (Hamann), Dunne, Ball, Ireland, Richards, Johnson, Petrov, Elano, (Sturridge), Jo (Evans)
Subs: Schmeichel (GK), Garrido, Fernandes, Caicedo

PRESS VIEW

Manchester City qualified for the first round of the Uefa Cup thanks to Joe Hart's heroics in the penalty shoot-out against Danish side FC Midtjylland.

The goalkeeper made great saves from Jonas Borring and Kolja Afriyie to give City a 4-2 victory on penalties after they went close to being dumped out.

Danny Califf's injury time own goal gave City a lifeline after what was a poor display during the 90 minutes. **(BBC)**

PLAYER & MANAGEMENT QUOTES

We deserved to win. **(Thomas Thomasberg, Midtjylland boss)**

I'm delighted, we showed a lot of character and I saw qualities and values in the team that I really liked. (**Mark Hughes**)

The nerves are fine now. It was really tough but we worked hard and deserved the goal. God gave us this lucky goal. (**Vedran Corluka**)

> ### Hart-stopping hero hauls City to safety
> Mark Hughes embryonic UEFA Cup bid had to rely on a nail biting penalty shoot-out as Manchester City kept their nerve to avoid an embarrassing defeat in the drizzle of Jutland. Vedran Corluka converted the winning spot kick with what could be his last kick for the club if Tottenham have their way, while goal keeper Joe Hart pushed his growing England claims with two brilliant saves.
>
> But lacklustre City needed the gift of a last minute own goal from hapless American defender Danny Califf to take this qualifying round tie into extra time.
>
> Midtjylland may have tumbled recently from the top of the Danish League but they were still head and shoulders above City for a worryingly long spell. Just as they had at Eastland's in a first leg they won with a goal from Danny Olsen, the Black Wolves often had more bite and the sharper football against a City side that struggled to spark. The Danes were calling the shots and it needed last-gasp defending to make sure they did not land the goal that would have made City's mission an uphill task.
>
> City's game needed to step up and there was more passion and desire about their start to the second half. Young striker Evans came on for Jo ten minutes from time as City tried to rescue the situation and Midtjylland held their heads in their hands when a Evans wayward header deflected off Califf into his own goal in the 90th minute.

SUPPORTERS' TALES

With all the European trips coming thick and fast, we decided a different and cheaper approach was required to get to see City play in Denmark again.

So rather than opting for one of the slightly overpriced day trips. The modes of transport went as follows

National express coach from Manchester via Birmingham to arrive at London Gatwick for 4.30 a.m.

Sterling airways Gatwick to Billund, then rounding up some fellow Blues at the airport in Denmark for a minibus ride to Herning and our hotel The Scandic Regina, with rumours that was the hotel the players were using, well there were plenty of suits in there, but all with UEFA badges but no players, so that was a false dawn. The Scandic was right in the heart of the City, so after a quick wash and change it was out to explore the delights of Herning town centre, a quick bite to eat in a restaurant and then to taste the local beverage, as by now the organised day trips had arrived.

Well at least they were guaranteed to find the ground courtesy of their coaches; we had not even given it a thought.

Chatter amongst fellow Blues soon discovered there was a train station nearby that went in the vicinity of the ground, well it stopped at some unmanned station with no platform but at least you could see the ground.

The story of the game we all know, with it being decided on penalties. The local police told us there would be buses back to the town centre, but they must have been invisible so we proceeded back to the station and not being fluent in Danish had no idea when the next one was due, so followed the train line in the direction we had come from, a nice one hour walk in the drizzle back to our hotel and a quick stop at the Herning Pizza Kebab House.

Oh and the return journey: two local buses to Billund Airport, flight to Dublin and then Dublin to Manchester. An adventure but give me a day trip anytime.

Tuborg! Carlsberg! Hvidtol (Part 1)

The 2008/09 European season saw City drawn against 3 Danish teams. FC Midtjylland in the qualifiers, Copenhagen in the last 32 and Aalborg in the last 16 of the competition!

FC Midtjylland was the first European trip I had attended and the story starts in Liverpool the week before the game. City trailed 1 nil from the first leg, a surprise home defeat. I was in Liverpool fast tracking my passport for the return leg in Herning. Four hours later I was in Manchester, passport in hand packing for the trip that was fast approaching.

We had booked a flight to Billund airport and then arranged a taxi with a few other city fans from Billund airport to Herning. We arrived at the hotel and quickly got our bearings. The game was that evening and we had a quick look around the town before jumping on a train towards the ground. The train stop was in the middle of nowhere but really close to the ground. Walking across the car park towards the ground the first thing that struck me was how similar the FC Midtjylland logo was to that of Charlton Athletics'.

We queued up waiting to be let in to the ground and as more City fans filtered towards the line of stewards waiting to search us news broke that Shaun Wright Phillips had resigned with the club creating a vibrant and buzzing atmosphere in the away end, to which the Danish stewards were totally bemused with the sudden joyous reactions of the City following. Within no time it was kick off and the game had begun, from what I remember we started really slowly and actually never looked like scoring. A really underwhelming performance from our team. I was stood by the wall in the middle of the away end with the tensions within the City fans camp about to reach the boil, Ched Evans was thrown on and almost instantaneously it paid off as a Michael Ball whipped in a cross and while under pressure from Evans, Danny Califf headed past his own keeper to send the fans into pandemonium. It felt like we had won the champions league, we celebrated for what seemed an eternity. The truth was the game had only just begun as we had to go through extra time and even penalties.

Extra time was a different story as City dominated the play trying to grab another goal, Daniel Sturridge smashing a shot against the cross bar in the process. The tie eventually went to penalties and was won after Joe Hart saved one and Vedran Corluka scored the following City penalty to send the players and fans home happy!

The game was over but the trip was still at an early stage, we walked back from the SAS Arena along the train tracks to the hotel, happy as anything, we had won and Shaun Wright Phillips had returned. There was no reason to be down.

The next day we woke and left the hotel after filling up on scrambled eggs and plenty of Danish bacon, after all we had a long day ahead of us. We jumped on a coach to Billund but had to change coach in the middle of nowhere, it took a good few hours to reach the airport and we made it just in time to catch the draw for the next round where we were drawn against FC Omonia of Cyprus.

Billund airport itself is very small; in fact it's just a room the size of a small sports hall. We were sat in a café eating Danish beef sat next to a pilot who was supposed to be flying a plane to the Faroe Islands but for some reason the plane had not arrived at the airport and no one knew where it was. It was all quite amusing really and it killed a lot of time listening to them trying to track down the plane. **(Daniel Waldon)**

AC OMONIA 1   MANCHESTER CITY 2

Goal Scorer: Jo (2)
UEFA Cup
First Round – First Leg, Thursday 18 September 2008
GSP Stadium, Nicosia, Cyprus
Attendance: 15,907

City Team:
Hart, Zabaleta, Dunne, Richards, Garrido, Ireland, Kompany (Fernandes), Elano (Hamann), Wright-Phillips, Jo (Sturridge), Robinho
Subs: Schmeichel (GK), M Ball, Ben-Haim, Evans

PRESS VIEW

Jo scored twice as Manchester City came from behind to beat Omonia in the first leg of their Uefa Cup first-round tie.

The Brazilian missed an open goal from six yards and hit the post as City wasted several first-half chances.

Stephen Ireland also hit the woodwork before Klodian Duro smashed Omonia ahead with a free-kick after half-time.

Jo fired against the bar before tapping in Shaun Wright-Phillips' pass to level, then met Pablo Zabaleta's cross soon after to slot home City's winner. **(BBC)**

Stamina, skill and patience will be the key factors that identify the winners of this seasons UEFA Cup and City are shaping up as though they have all three elements in their armoury. (*Manchester Evening News*)

MANAGEMENT VIEW

Jo worked really hard for the team and I am delighted he got his reward. They were two good finishes and he will settle down now.

It is important for a striker at a new club to get off the mark and make an impression and he did that.

Omonia worked extremely hard and are a decent side. We knew we had to play well and there is still work to be done in the return match.

However we are in a strong position, especially as we have away goals on the board.

I thought we gave a professional performance in Europe and got the job done in the end. **(Mark Hughes)**

MANCHESTER CITY 2   AC OMONIA 1

Goal Scorers: Elano, Wright-Phillips
UEFA Cup
First Round – Second Leg, Thursday 2 October 2008
City of Manchester Stadium
Attendance: 25,304

City Team: Hart, Zabaleta, Ben-Haim, Richards, Garrido, Wright-Phillips, Ireland, Kompany (Hamann), Elano, Robinho (Petrov), Jo (Evans)
Subs: Schmeichel (GK), Ball, Fernandes, Sturridge

PRESS VIEW

Second-half goals from Elano and Shaun Wright-Phillips sank Omonia Nicosia and made sure of Manchester City's progress into the group stages of the Uefa Cup.

City were poor in the first half but Elano broke the deadlock soon after the break, meeting a Robinho pass with a bullet shot into the bottom corner.

Wright-Phillips made it 2-0 soon after, firing home after riding two tackles.

Rasheed Alabi replied with a late header for Omonia but City still completed a routine 4-2 aggregate win. **(BBC)**

Shaun Wright-Phillips enhanced his chances of an England recall after a half time rollicking from Mark Hughes sparked Manchester City into the UEFA Cup group stages. **(*Daily Mail*)**

After a slow start City cruised into the group stages thanks to some Brazilian brilliance. Sparky's boys were a class act and never looked like losing. **(*Sun*)**

Sleepy Manchester City woke up with a start and hit Omonia with some Premier League style football in the second half. **(*Daily Star*)**

Party Time. SWP loves Samba beat

A pair of Brazilians and an Englishman who would not look out of place in the famous yellow shirt have ensured Manchester City's European adventure goes on.

It had been a terribly dull first half until a few choice words at the break from Mark Hughes clearly sparked City into life. Three minutes into the restart and Robinho broke down the left flank before rolling the ball back for Elano. His strike with the outside of his right foot from 25 yards was unstoppable and arrowed into the bottom left hand corner. It was two, seven minutes later with creator supreme Robinho at the centre of things again. He played the ball out wide to Pablo Zabaleta and the full back in turn found Wright-Phillips just inside the box. The winger forced his way through two challenges before volleying in.

The visitor's grabbed a 78th minute consolation through sub Rasheed Alabi to the delight of their vociferous fans.

PLAYER & MANAGEMENT VIEW

Once we got the goal it was comfortable. It's great for the players the fans and the whole club to qualify for the group stages of the UEFA Cup. (**Shaun Wright-Phillips**)

We want to get more experience in Europe and we are now looking forward to four more group fixtures. (**Mark Hughes**)

MANCHESTER CITY 3   FC TWENTE 2

Goal Scorers: Wright-Phillips, Robinho, Benjani
UEFA Cup
Group Stage, Thursday 6 November 2008
City of Manchester Stadium
Attendance: 21,247

City Team: Hart, Zabaleta, Dunne, Richards, Garrido, Wright-Phillips, Vassell (Elano), Fernandes, Ireland, Robinho, Jo (Benjani)
Subs: Schmeichel (GK), Onuoha, Ben Haim, Hamann, Evans

PRESS VIEW

A stunning Robinho strike helped Manchester City see off a spirited FC Twente side in Group A of the Uefa Cup.

Shaun-Wright Phillips put City ahead with a low shot but hesitant home defending allowed Eljero Elia to level.

City struggled until Robinho fired into the top corner after the break and Benjani's deflected shot made it 3-1.

But Rob Wielaert's header pulled a goal back for Twente and, after Robinho hit the post twice for City, a late miss by Stein Huysegems cost Twente a point. **(BBC)**

MANAGEMENT VIEW

Robinho could have had a hat-trick. But we were grateful for the strike for the second goal. He has fantastic ability in those areas.

He is one of the best players I have seen in that position to be able to manipulate the ball and create things inside the box.

Overall, we are delighted. We have got a positive result and that is what we need to achieve at home to progress. **(Mark Hughes)**

We felt we should have got something from the game. We certainly had chances.

But the character of the players was magnificent after we went a goal down so early against City's front five.

We dug in, and it was end to end. It was an open game, which must have been great for the neutral – but for both managers it was edge-of-the-seat stuff. **(Steve McLaren, FC Twente boss)**

SCHALKE 0   MANCHESTER CITY 2

Goal Scorers: Benjani, Ireland

UEFA Cup
Group Stage, Thursday 27 November 2008
Veltins Arena, Gelsenkirchen, Germany
Attendance: 54,142

City Team: Hart, Richards, Kompany, Dunne, Garrido (Ball), Wright-Phillips, Vassell, Hamann, Ireland, Sturridge, Benjani (Jo)
Subs: Schmeichel, Ben Haim, Logan, Berti, Evans

Manchester City booked their place in the last 32 of the Uefa Cup with an impressive victory away at Schalke.

PRESS VIEW

Jermaine Jones was twice denied by City goalkeeper Joe Hart in the first half as the home side started brightly.

However, it was the visitors who went in front as Daniel Sturridge burst down the left flank before crossing for Benjani to finish from six yards.

Stephen Ireland had a goal ruled out for offside before he capped an all action display with City's second.

England's recent superiority over Germany on the football field was emphatically reinforced by the buoyant Blues, and there was no fluke about this stroll in front of a packed Veltins Arena, for the hard working, slick passing, well organised Blues were far and away the better side. **(*Manchester Evening News*)**

Hughes is hailing City's united front

The PA announcer at the stadium mistakenly called City's fans 'Manchester United' supporters when announcing details of their post-match transport and at times they must have thought they were watching European experts United as City produced the kind of football associated with their rivals.

Mark Hughes was delighted and said "We always looked strong on the break and our performance was excellent. The work rate from the whole team from start to finish was really excellent, but everyone did their jobs well and put in a massive amount of work".

Striker Benjani started the victory march in the 32nd minute when he powered City ahead, Stephen Ireland then struck in the 67th minute, slotting the ball home to send the travelling City fans into a raucous rendition of 'Blue Moon'.

Schalke had begun the game with an unbeaten home record against English clubs and came close on a number of occasions but it was pressure City more than adequately copped with on a night that virtually guaranteed their further progress in the competition.

MANAGEMENT QUOTES

I thought we were really comfortable and knew when to break, so as a consequence Schalke were always on the back foot. It was a very accomplished performance. (**Mark Hughes**)

I think the defeat is justified. The disappointment is there even if we have played a very good team. In the last half hour we lacked belief in a draw or a victory. (**Fred Rutten, Schalke coach**)

SUPPORTERS' TALES

Our day started nice and early, checking in at 4.45 a.m. for the 6.45 a.m. Thomas Cook day trip to Shalke via Cologne.

Two and half hours later and after our standard microwaved breakfast (Omelette, Sausage, Beans, Bread Roll, Orange Juice) and the efficient distribution of match tickets, we were on our coaches heading to Cologne City centre.

So with match ticket in hand, what could go wrong, well we will come to that a bit later. The day went well as City fans mingled in amongst the bars and because it was fast approaching Christmas time, the seasonal markets, sampling the local beverages and food.

Five coach loads of supporters were ready (well almost as some struggled to find the coaches in their drunken haze) to depart at 16.00 ready for an estimated one hour transfer to the ground.

CITY
LEAGUE CHAMPIONS

WEDNESDAY SEPTEMBER 18th 1968
Kick-off 7-45 p.m.

VERSUS
FENERBAHCE S.K. Champions of Turkey

MANCHESTER CITY FOOTBALL CLUB LTD.
European Champion Clubs' Cup
OFFICIAL PROGRAMME ONE SHILLING

MANCHESTER CITY NEWS 1/-

VERSUS
ACADEMICA DE COIMBRA
EUROPEAN CUP WINNERS' CUP
4th Finals — 2nd Leg
WEDNESDAY
18th MARCH 1970
Kick-off 7-30 p.m.

MANCHESTER CITY NEWS 1/-

VERSUS
F.C. SCHALKE '04
EUROPEAN CUP WINNERS' CUP
Semi-Finals — 2nd Leg
WEDNESDAY 15th APRIL 1970
Kick-off 7-45 p.m.

TONY BOOK — CAPTAIN
REINHARD LIBUDA — MANNSCHAFTSFUHRER

TAÇA DOS VENCEDORES DAS TAÇAS

ACADÉMICA
———
MANCHESTER CITY F. C.

QUARTOS DE FINAL

Seit 24 Jahren das aktuelle Fußball-Programm

Westdeutsche Sonder Vorschau

FUSSBALL-STADION-BLATT

Jahrgang 25　　1. April 1970　　Preis: 20 Pf.

Schalke will ins Europa-Cup-Endspiel:
- MSV Duisburg – 1. FC Köln
- RW Essen – Bor. M.-Gladb.
- Viktoria Köln – VfL Bochum

Schalke 04 - Manchester City

Reinhard Libuda, Schalke 04.
Klaus Fichtel, Schalke 04.

Gerüstbau Arnholdt, Gelsenk., Ruf 73011

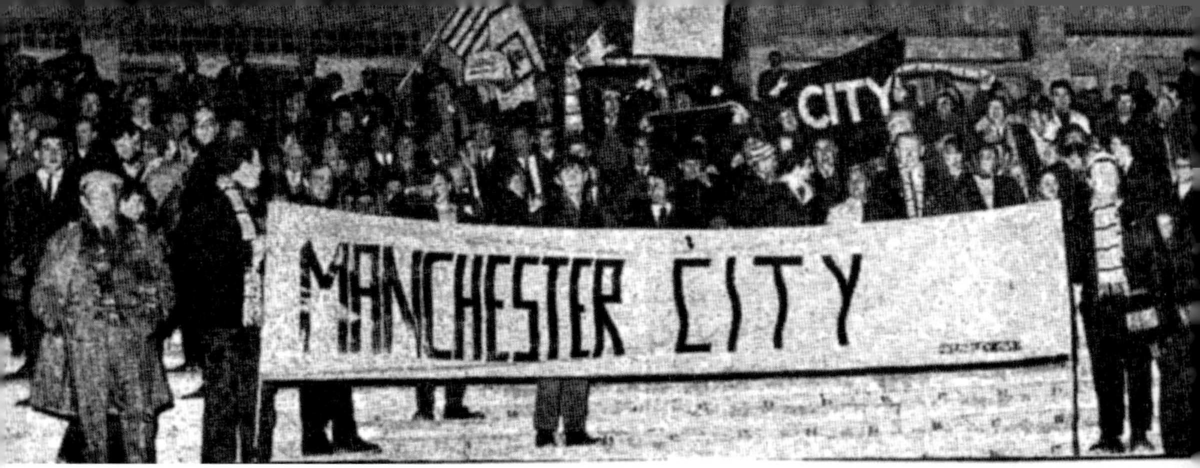
CITY
MANCHESTER CITY

FRANCIS
COLIN
FILTERCIGARETTEN

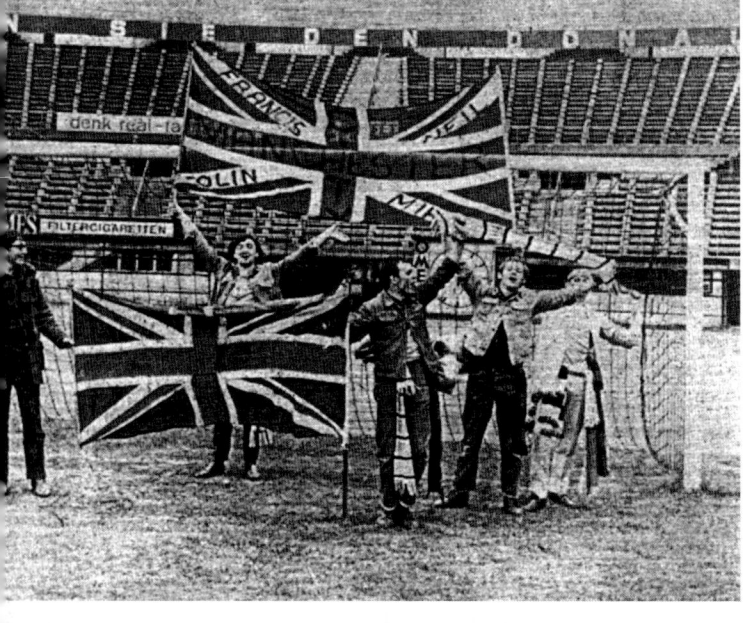

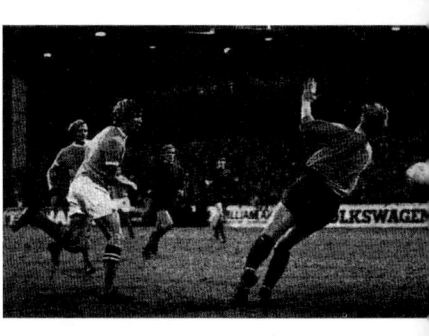

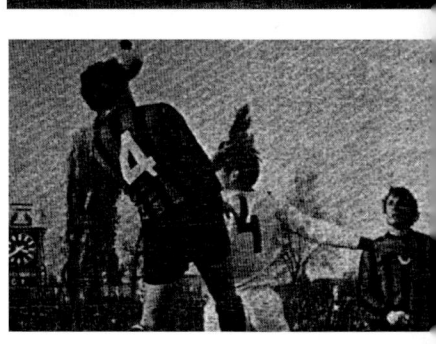

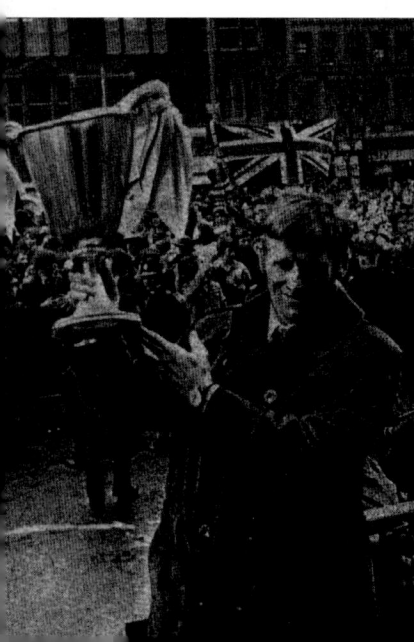

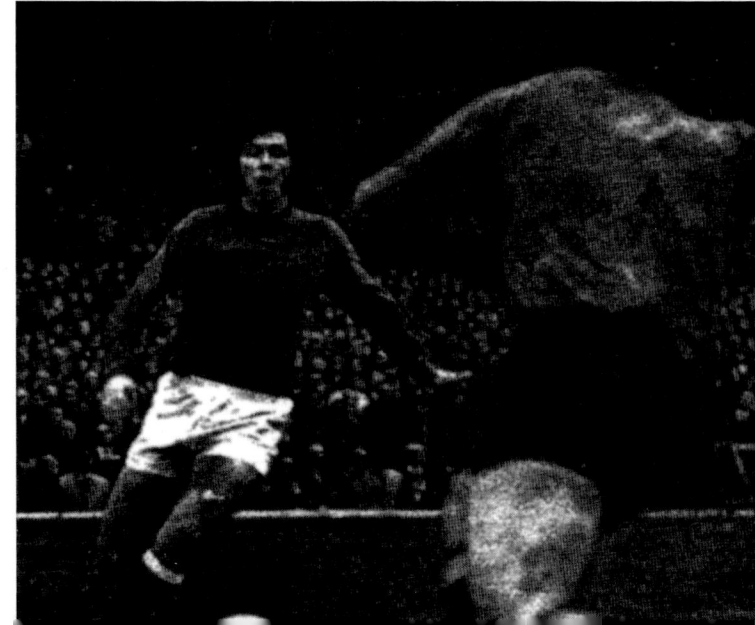

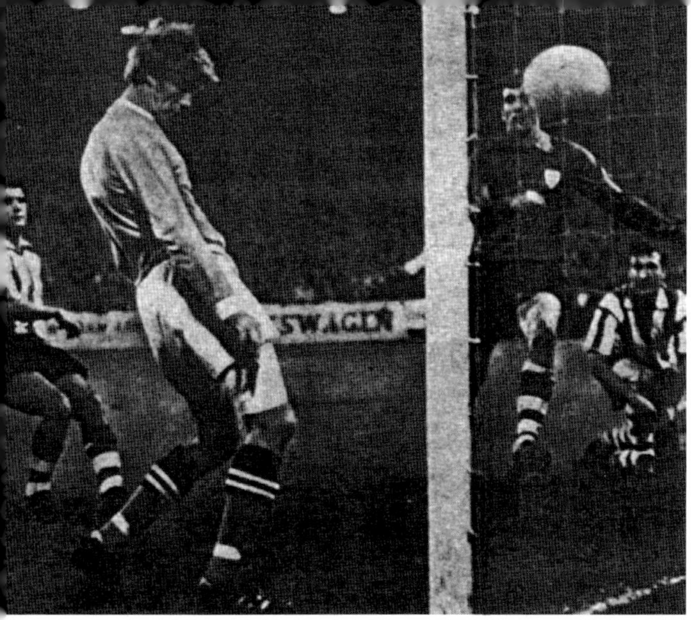
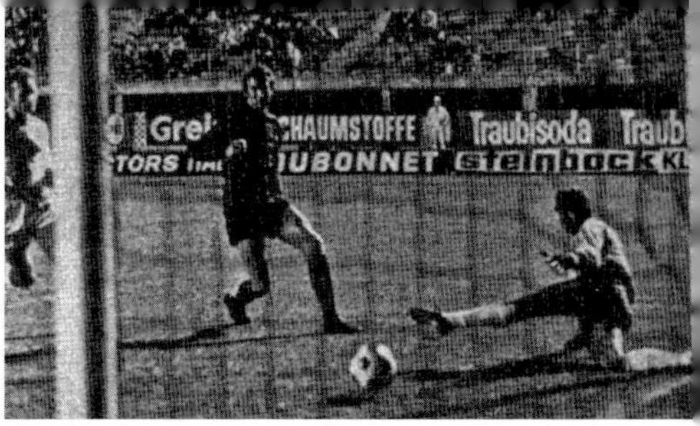
SCHAUMSTOFFE
Traubisoda
DUBONNET
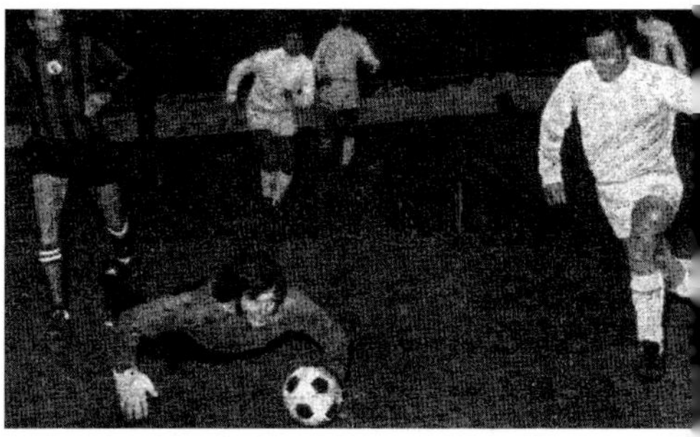
IBERIA

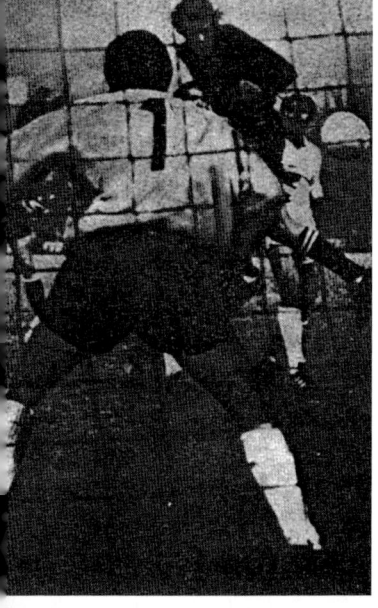

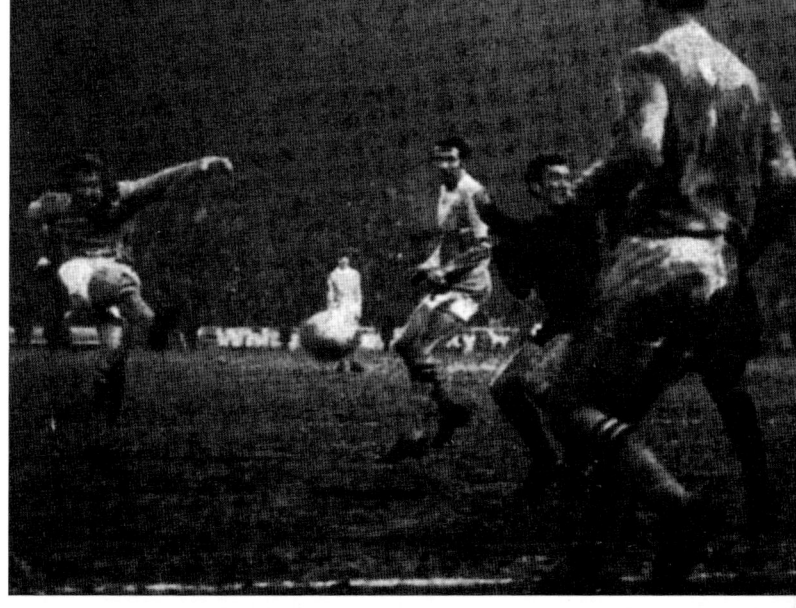

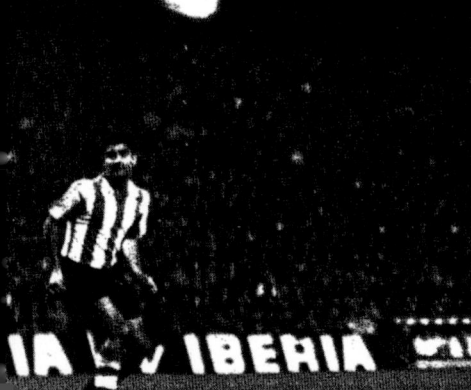

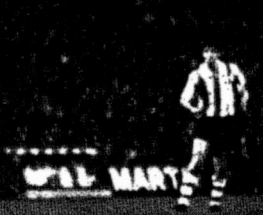

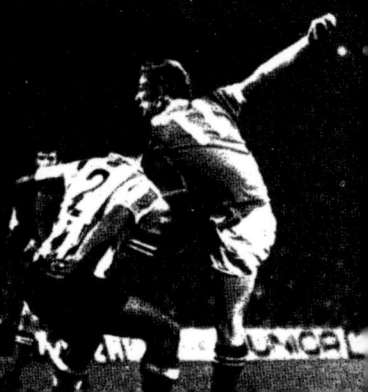

CHELSEA

 **FOOTBALL CLUB**

v

MANCHESTER CITY

European Cup-Winners' Cup, Semi-Final (First Leg) Season 1970-71

Wednesday, 14th April, 1971—Kick-off 7.45 p.m.

OFFICIAL PROGRAMME 5p (1/-)

MANCHESTER CITY

NEWS 5p

VERSUS
CHELSEA
EUROPEAN CUP WINNERS' CUP
SEMI-FINALS 2nd LEG
WEDNESDAY
28th APRIL 1971
Kick-off 7-45 p.m.

WELCOME CHELSEA FROM OUR CHAIRMAN

MR A. V. ALEXANDER

TONIGHT we are hosts to Chelsea, one of the great British clubs. It would have been nice to meet them in Athens for the Final. But whatever happens at least Britain will have one team there. I am certain you will extend your usual magnificent Mancunian hospitality. And may the better team win!

MANCHESTER CITY

NEWS 1/- 5p

VERSUS
LINFIELD
OF BELFAST
EUROPEAN CUP WINNERS' CUP
16th FINALS—1st LEG
WEDNESDAY
16th SEPTEMBER 1970
Kick-off 7-45 p.m.

ALL ALONE: Colin Bell heads in the second goal against Bilbao on the way to last year's Cup Winners' Cup Final. *Picture: Daily Express*

MANCHESTER CITY

NEWS 1/- 5p

VERSUS
HONVED
OF HUNGARY
EUROPEAN CUP WINNERS' CUP
8th FINALS—2nd LEG
WEDNESDAY
4th NOVEMBER 1970
Kick-off 7-45 p.m.

HATS OFF TO CITY: A smiling Joe Mercer returns to Manchester after that victorious first leg. *Picture: Daily Mirror*

MANCHESTER CITY

NEWS 5p

VERSUS
GORNIK ZABRZE
OF POLAND
EUROPEAN CUP WINNERS' CUP
QUARTER FINALS 2nd LEG
WEDNESDAY
24th MARCH 1971
Kick-off 7-45 p.m.

DANGER MAN ... the Gornik star who sets Soccer alight wherever he plays ... Lubanski, pride of all Poland.

U.E.F.A. CUP - First round - First leg

MANCHESTER CITY

v

JUVENTUS
TORINO

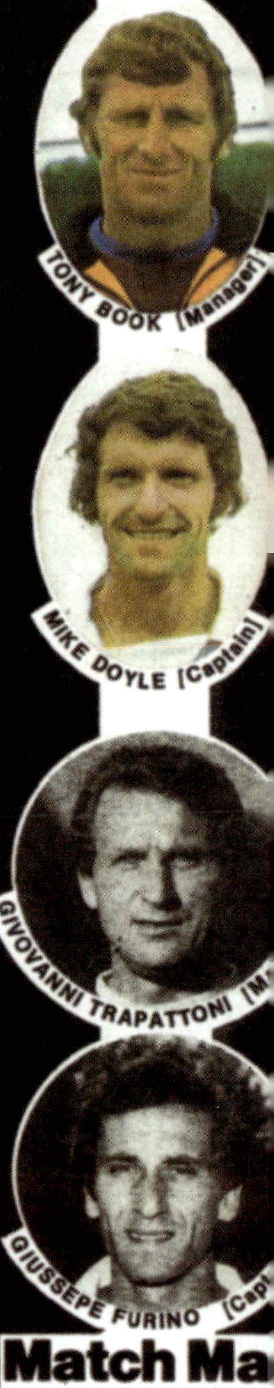

TONY BOOK (Manager)

MIKE DOYLE (Captain)

GIOVANNI TRAPATTONI (M)

GIUSSEPE FURINO (Cap)

Match Ma

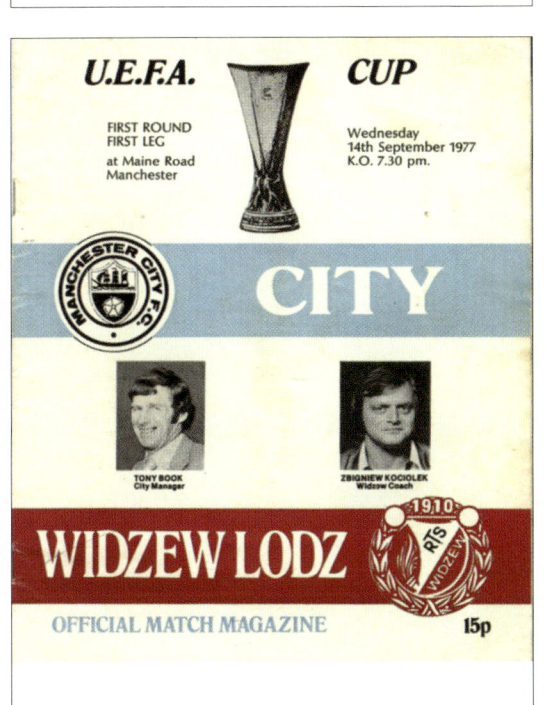

ACTION IN ENSCHEDE
UEFA CUP
1st Round 1st Leg

U.E.F.A. CUP THIRD ROUND Second Leg at Maine Road, Manchester Kick-off 7-30 p.m.

Wednesday, September 27th 1978   **U.E.F.A. CUP**   at Maine Road, Manchester

 TONY BOOK (Manager)
 DAVE WATSON (Captain)
 EPI DROST (Captain)
 ANTON 'Spitz' KOHN (Team Manager)

 CITY

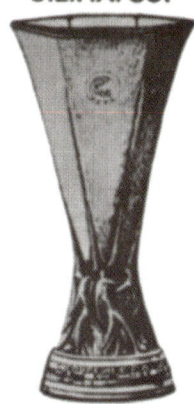
FIRST ROUND SECOND LEG

 F.C. TWENTE

KICK-OFF 7-30 p.m.

MATCH MAGAZINE 20p

ACTION in SAN SIRO

Wednesday, December 6th, 1978

U.E.F.A. CUP 3rd Round, 1st Leg 23-11-78

MATCH MAGAZINE: PRICE 20p.

U.E.F.A. CUP

WEDNESDAY, OCTOBER 18th 1978

TONY BOOK (Manager)

DAVE WATSON (Captain)

MANCHESTER CITY v STANDARD LIEGE

SECOND ROUND FIRST LEG

ROBERT WASEIGE (Chief Coach)

CHRISTIAN LABARBE (Captain)

KICK-OFF 7-30 p.m.

AT MAINE ROAD MANCHESTER

MATCH MAGAZINE 20p

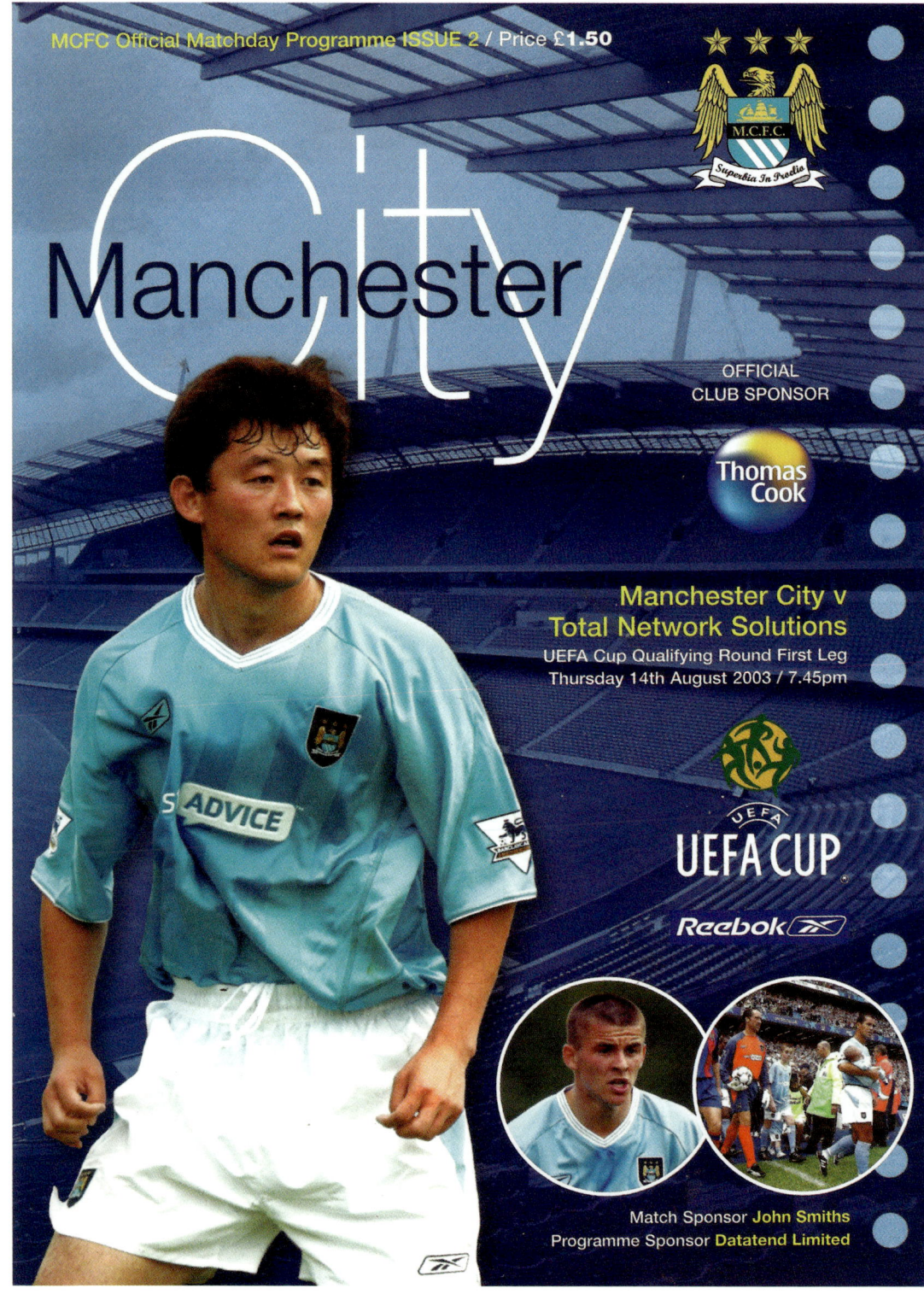

TOTAL NETWORK SOLUTIONS
FOOTBALL CLUB

TOTAL NETWORK SOLUTIONS
v
MANCHESTER CITY

UEFA Cup Preliminary Round
Second Leg
Millennium Stadium Cardiff
28 August 2003 / 7.45 pm

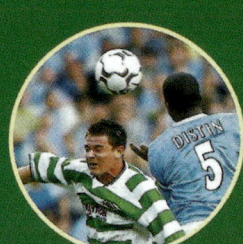

SHIRT SPONSOR

OFFICIAL KIT SUPPLIER

MATCH SPONSOR
J T HUGHES MITSUBISHI
MATCHBALL SPONSOR
WALKER SMITH WAY
Solicitors
PROGRAMME SPONSOR
ZYCKO

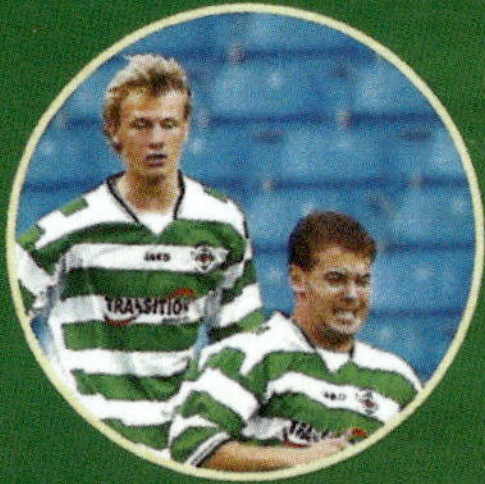

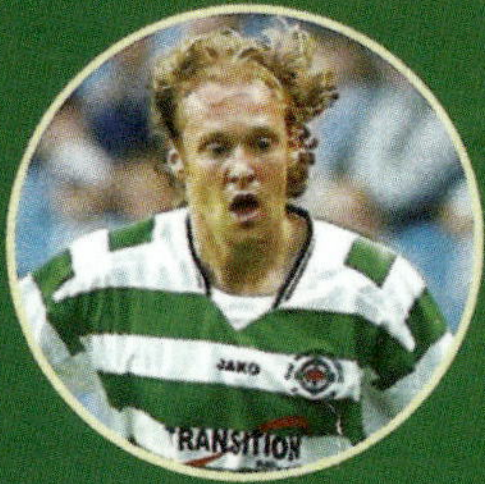

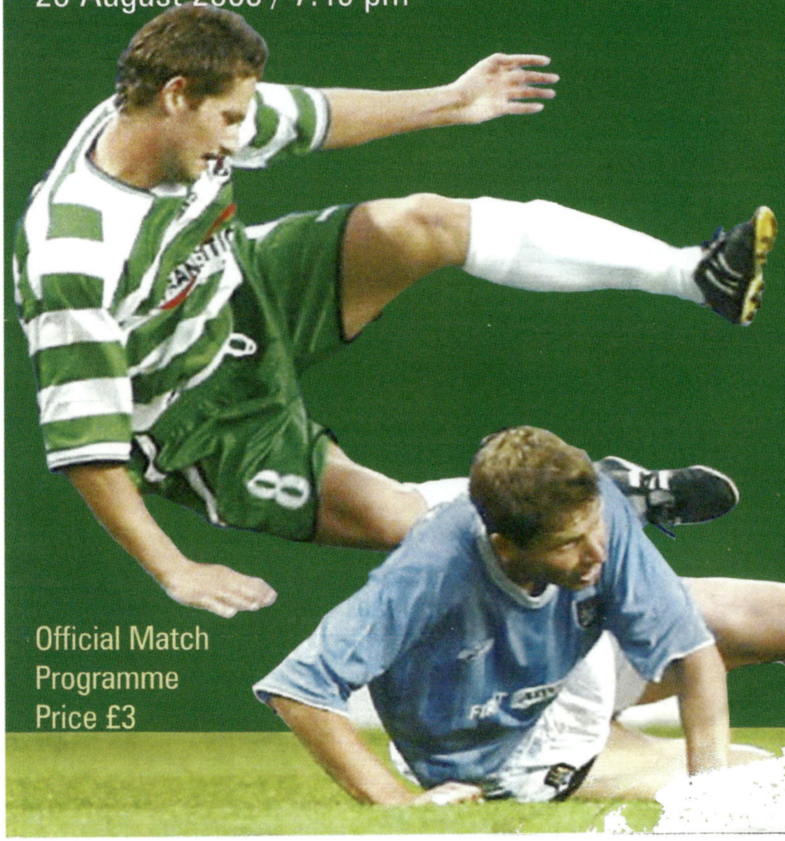

Official Match
Programme
Price £3

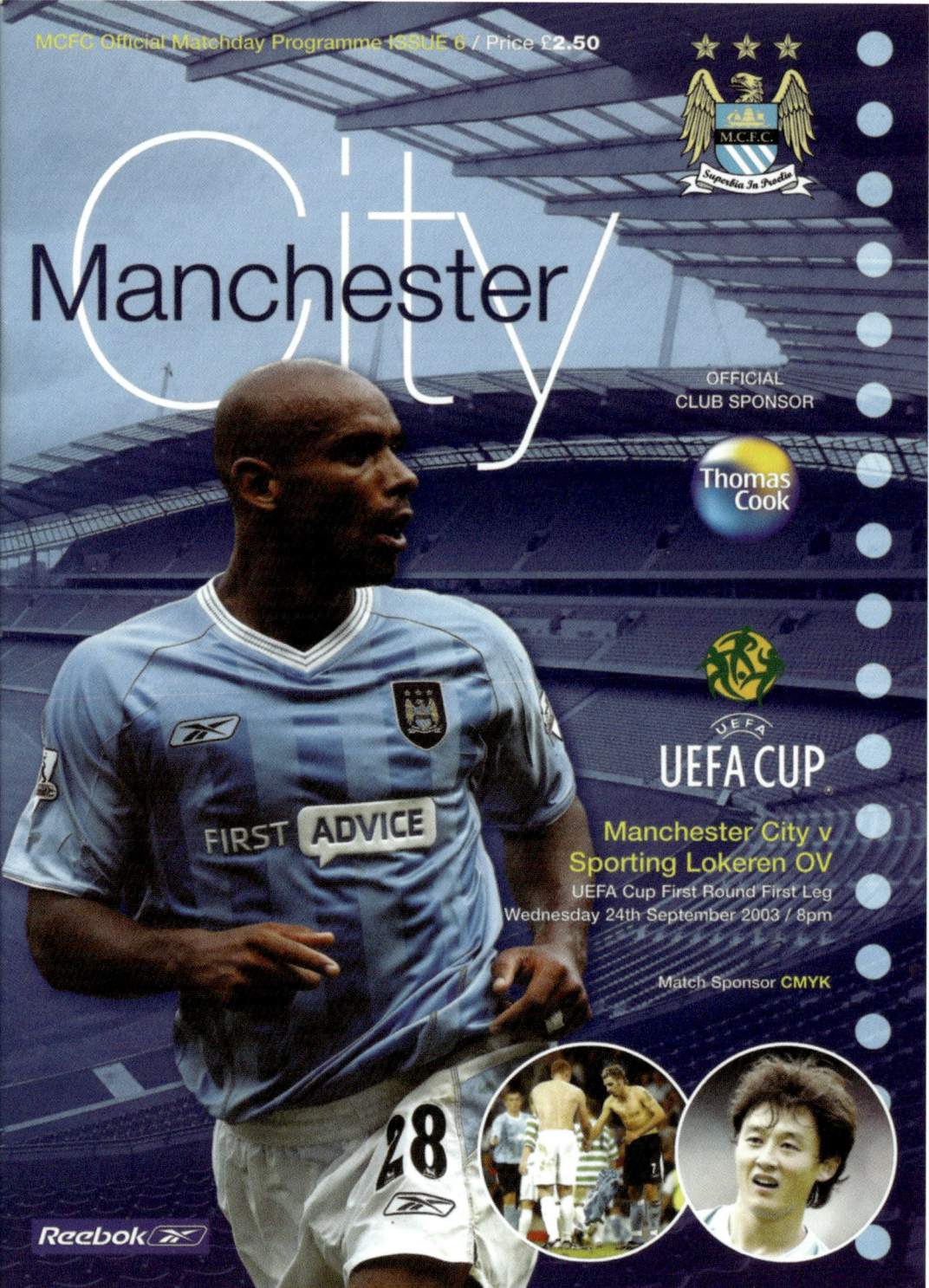

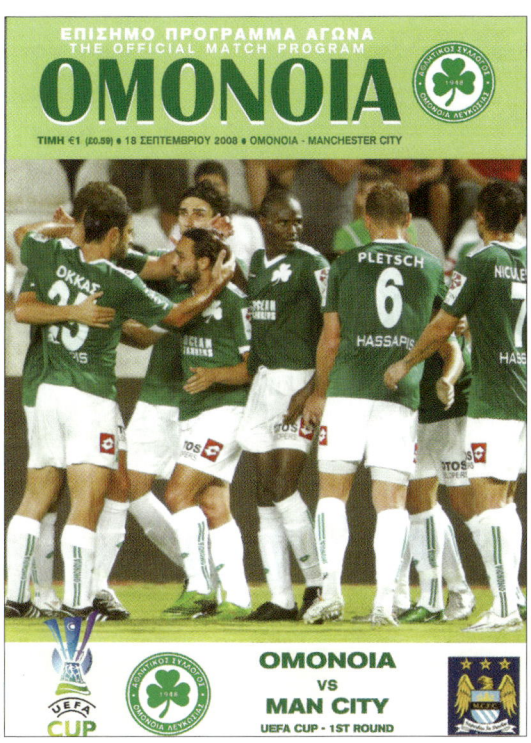

    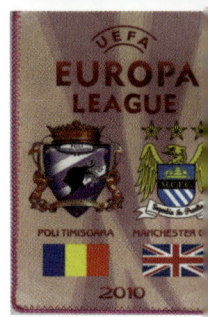

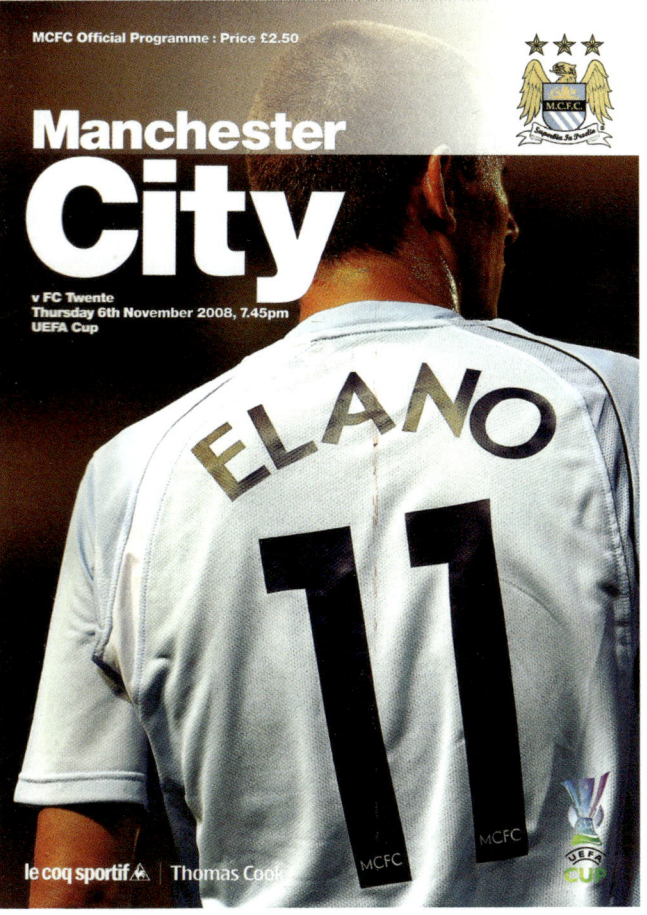

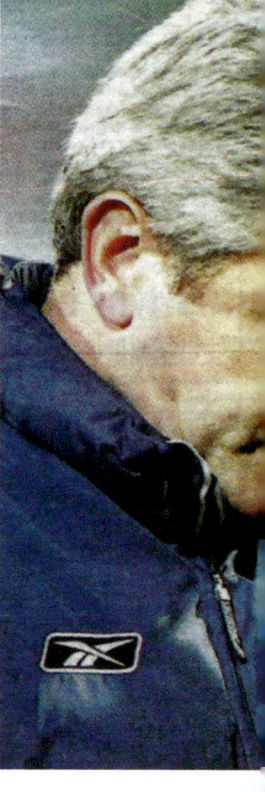

FC KØBENHAVN
MANCHESTER CITY
19 Februar 2009
UEFA Cuppen
1/16 Finaler
PARKEN STADION
Klokken 20.45

Round of 32 - 19 February 2009 20:05

Kobenhavn v Manchester City

STADIUM - PARKEN

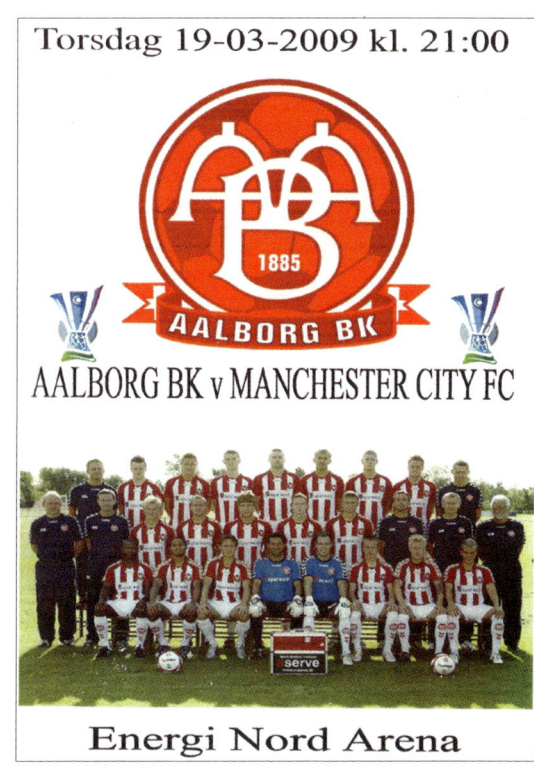

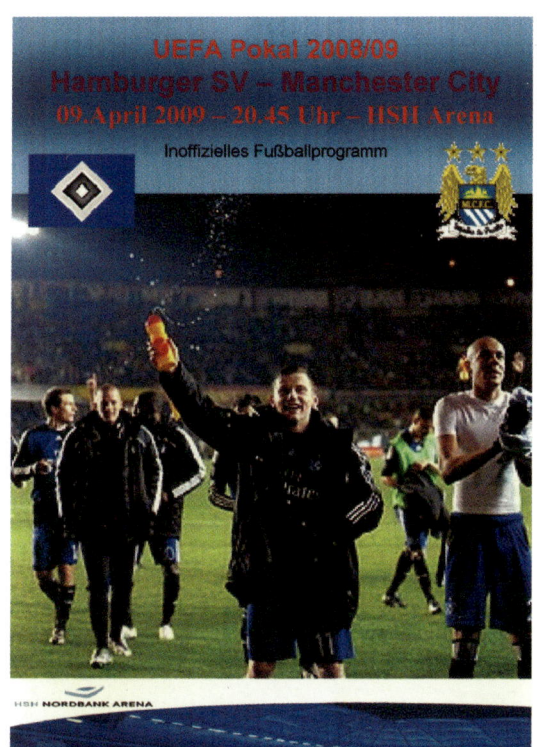

MCFC Official Programme : Price £3.00

Manchester City

v Hamburg SV
Thursday 16th April 2009, 7.45pm
UEFA Cup Quarter Final

le coq sportif | Thomas Cook

CUP

T: 0870 062 1894 W: mcfc.co.uk
MCFC v EB/Streymur COACH 10
Coach Travel to Oakwell Stadium
Thu 31st JUL 2008 DEPARTS 4.30pm
UEFA Cup Qualifying Round 1, 2nd Leg
Travel from City of Manchester Stadium
000000203250 Mr Andrew Waldon
8TEB10 SEAT 0027 PRICE £0.00
le coq sportif
TRAVEL PASS
PRICE £0.00

Stamnummer 30
BEKER DER BEKERHOUDERS
WOENSDAG 12 NOVEMBER 1969, te 20 uur
K. LIERSE S. K. — MANCHESTER CITY
(BELGIE)
(ENGELAND)
00197
RING : (Zitplaats)
VAK A
N° 197
PRIJS : 175 Fr

0227
Sp. Lokeren O-Vl. - Manchester City
Daknam Stadion
Wednesday 15th October 2003
Time 20u.30
1st round UEFA Cup

Gelsenkirchen trinkt
Glückauf-Bier
FC Gelsenkirchen-Schalke 04 e
1-0
02771
Europa-Pokalspiel
Schalke 04 – Manchester City
Mittwoch, 1. April 1970 - 20.00 Uhr
Stehplatz Gera
DM 5,50
einschl. Sportg
u. Mehrwertste
Aufbewahren und auf Verlange
gen. Keine Haftung für Sach- un
schäden. Kein Recht auf Rücke
Plätze müssen ½ Stunde vor Sp
eingenommen sein.

F.I.G.C. LEGA NAZIONALE SERIE A
SERIE A
MILAN
RISERVA A
DISTINTI CENTRALI
007148
Conservare per il controllo
CAMPIONATO NAZIONALE 78-79
Banca Popolare di Lecco

F.C. Maine Road · Manchester
MANCHESTER CITY F.C.
E.U.F.A. CUP
Season 1978-79
SECOND ROUND — FIRST LEG
CITY
versus
STANDARD LIEGE
Wednesday, 18th October 1978
Kick-off 7-30 p.m.
You are advised to take up your position
half an hour before the kick-off
K ROW 20 SEAT 15
North Stand £1.50
Secretary
E RETAINED (SEE PLAN AND CONDITIONS ON BACK).

WOSTIW
PEZP
STADION ŚLĄSKI
MANCHESTER CITY
GÓRNIK ZABRZE
10 MARCA 1971 R.
010987
CENA
zgpw k-ce, 169-71 38.500

CHELSEA
FOOTBALL AND ATHLETIC CO. LTD.
Admit to Directors' Stand
14 APR 1971
COMPLIMENTARY
CHELSEA
FOOTBALL & ATHLETIC CO. LTD.
CHELSEA V.
MAN. CITY
14 APR 1971
Admit to DIRECTORS' STAND
Row E Seat 20
COMPLIMENTARY
Secretary

CITY F.C. Maine Road · Mar
E.U.F.A. CUP QUARTER FINAL —
Manchester City
versus
Borussia Moenchengladb
Wednesday, 7th March 19
Kick-off 7-30 p.m.
You are advised to take up your pos
half an hour before the kick-off
BLOCK F ROW C SEAT

MAN-CHESTER CITY
GÓR-NIK ZABRZE

JUVENTUS
F.I.G.C. - LEGA NAZIONALE
TORINO - 29 SETTEMBRE 1976
JUVENTUS - MANCH
DISTINTI CEN

Robotnicze Towarzystwo Sportowe
„WIDZEW"
BEZPŁATNY
WIDZEW — MANCHESTER CITY
28.09.77
Nr biletu

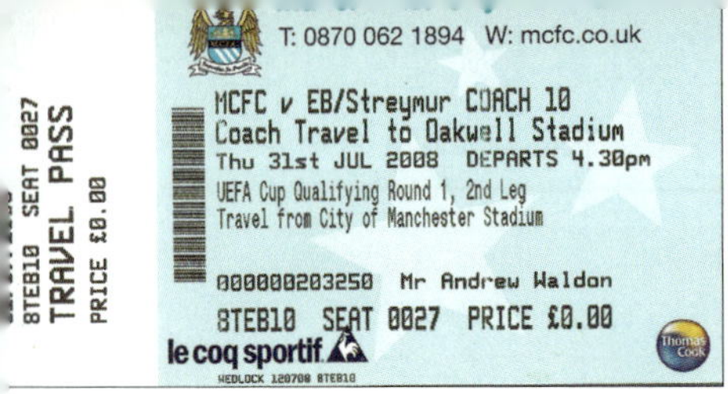

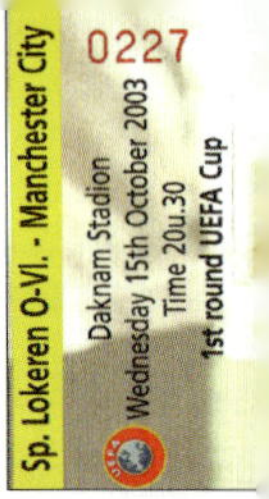

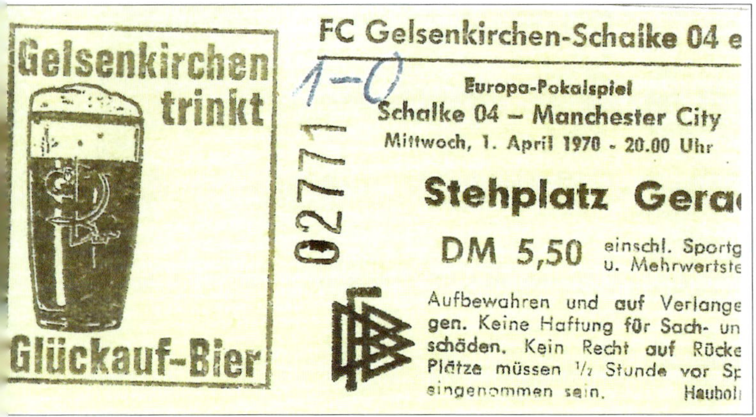

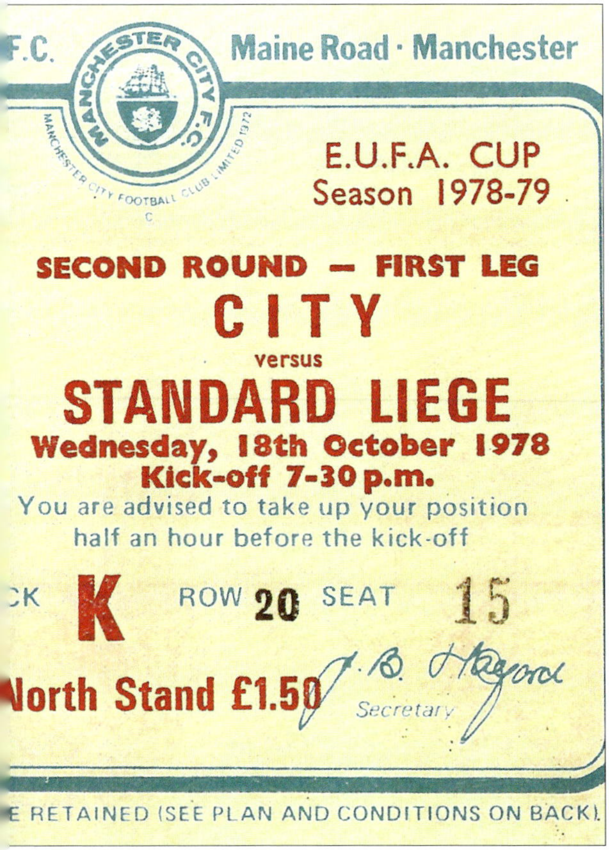

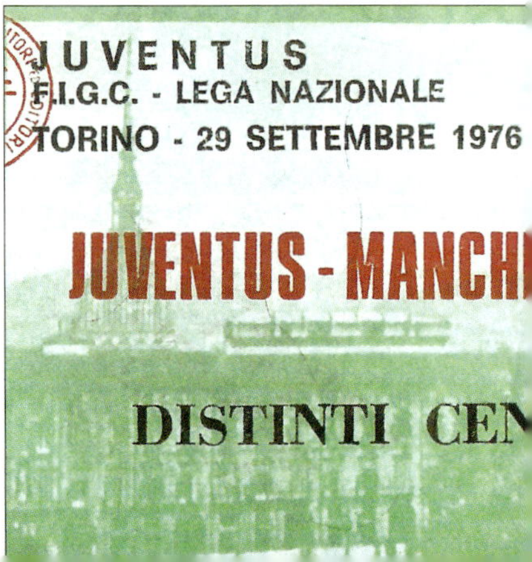

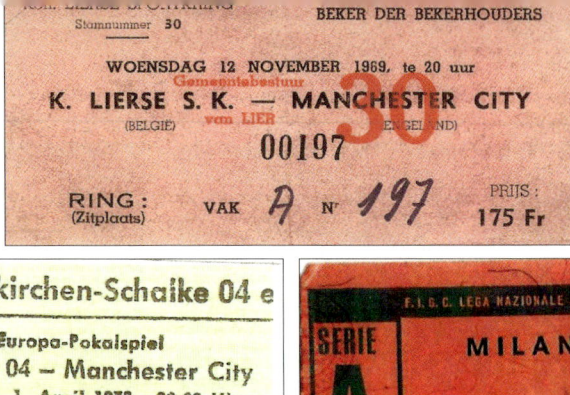

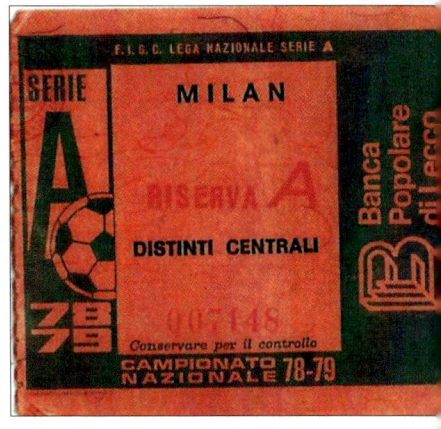

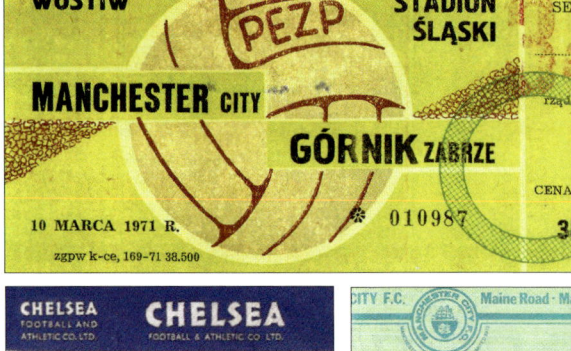

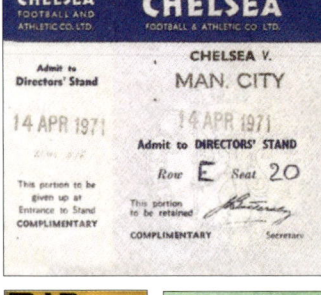

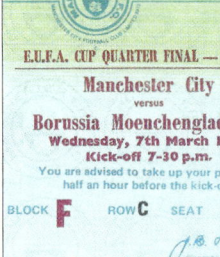

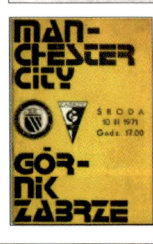

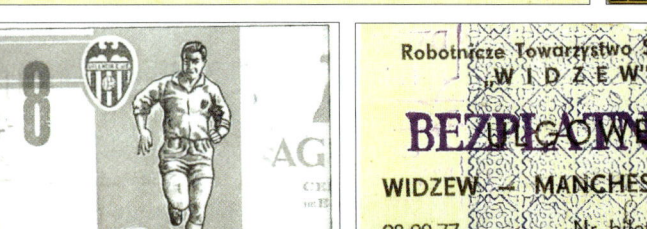

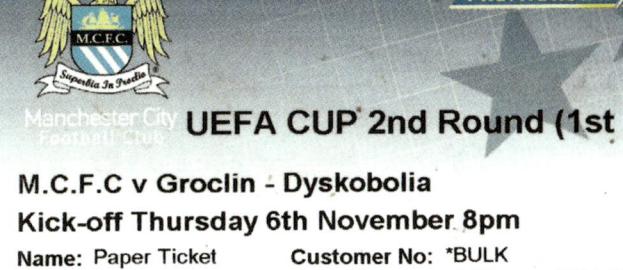

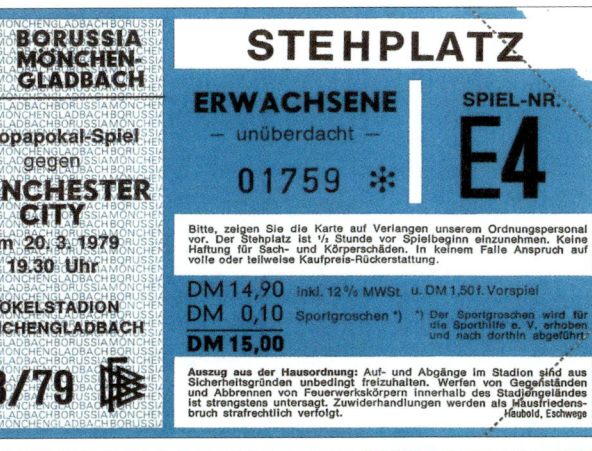

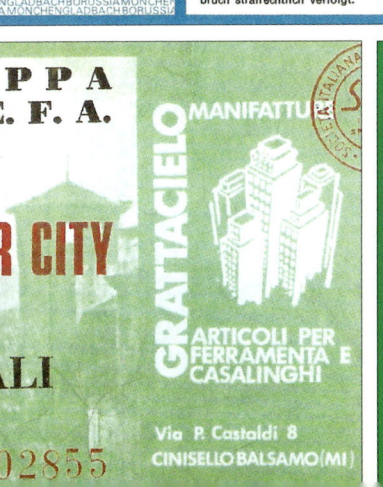

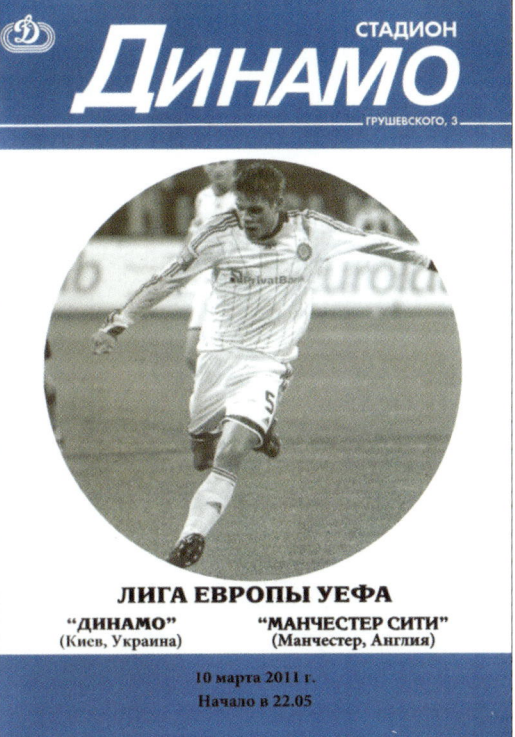

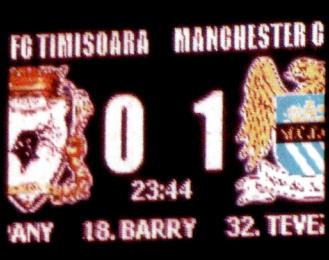

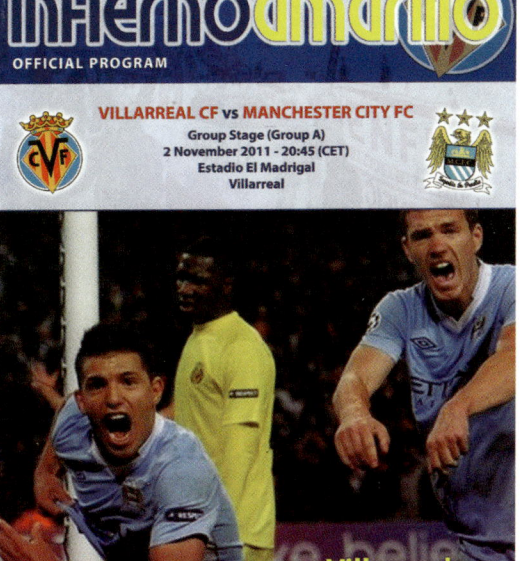

MCFC Official Programme
UCL 02 £3

Manchester City v Villarreal
Tuesday 18th October 2011 7.45pm

18:00 CET, 8 de março de 2012

SCP Vs Manchester City

 **VS**

STADIUM
ESTÁDIO JOSÉ ALVALADE
Rodada de 16, Uefa Liga Europa

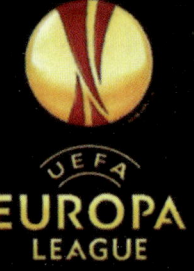

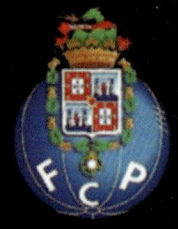

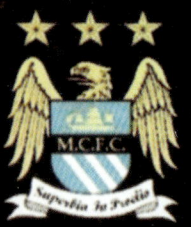

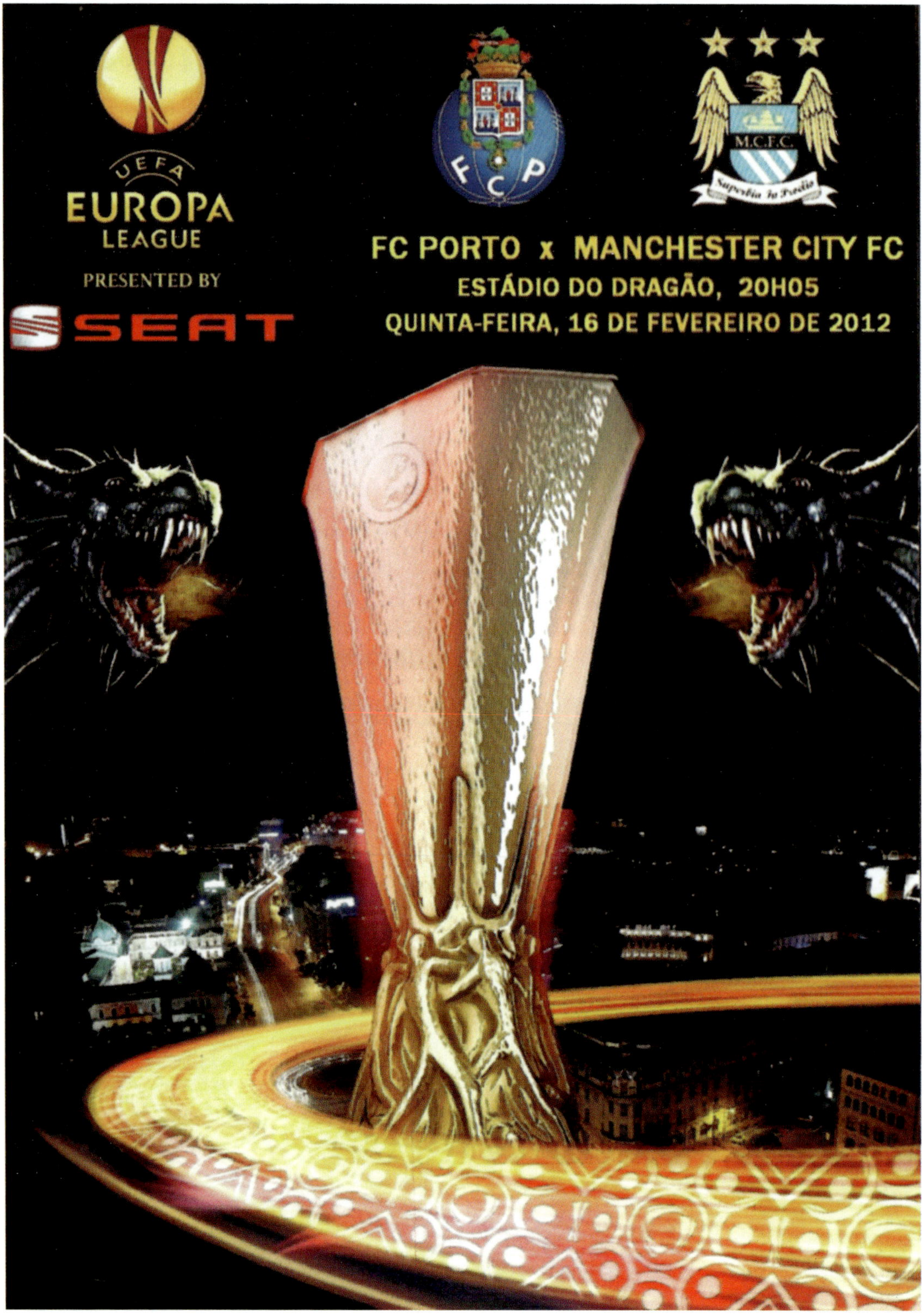
UEFA
EUROPA
LEAGUE
PRESENTED BY
SEAT
FCP
M.C.F.C.
Superbia in Proelio
FC PORTO x MANCHESTER CITY FC
ESTÁDIO DO DRAGÃO, 20H05
QUINTA-FEIRA, 16 DE FEVEREIRO DE 2012

Well who ever thought of this had severely underestimated German rush hour traffic on the Autobahn, although it was not helped by a couple of crashes and an unscheduled stop for a non-existent police escort.

The coach driver was asked that many times by supporters who were becoming increasingly frustrated and bemused, how far we were off, naturally he did not speak a word of English. So with five minutes to kick off and the coaches parked up a good distance from the ground, we were all running up a hill to try and make the start of the game.

Gasping for a drink on entrance, Schalke's Veltins Arena had invented this idea of being only able to make purchases using a 'Knappenkarte' smart card and you had to buy them from a separate stand. Faced with missing more of the game or dying of thirst, and having spent near on £300 to get there, the match action won my vote, good choice by me as City turned in one of their best European performances. **(Daniel Thomas)**

Schalke Auf Wiedersehen!

The Schalke away trip back in 2008 is one that sticks in my mind as the first real insight into City arriving on the European scene during my life time. Flying into Köln from Manchester we were dropped into the heart of Köln, allowed to explore the city at our will. It was late November and the Christmas Markets had just hit the city, a vibrant buzz swept through the air as coach by coach the city faithful gathered in the main square. Walking through the city and towards the Köln cathedral the bars on route started to pop up with City flags, the invasion had begun.

As the day started to fade into the night and the many market stalls and shops in Köln started to close. We, the City fans, made our way back to the coach pick up point ready to start the 40 mile journey to Gelsenkirchen, little did we know a nightmare was about to play out right in front of our eyes.

Around 20 minutes into the journey we hit major traffic, standstill. As the time passed anticipation for the game quickly turned to the sudden realisation that we may not make the game in time.

A fellow City fan, who spoke German, approached the driver and asked how far the coach was from Gelsenkirchen, and the stadium. '50 kilometres' was the response from the City fan translating for the rest of the fans on coach. We had 30 minutes to travel 50 kilometres and the traffic was still at a standstill. As time ticked on more fans became frustrated and concerned at the lack of movement. Then suddenly we started to move again, slowly. But we were getting there. Phone calls from the Thomas Cook reps on our coach to other reps on the other coaches soon pointed out that we had not been 50 kilometres from the ground but in fact 15 kilometres. The ground was in sight and the coaches made their way along the road to the stadium, the teams where in the tunnel and we hadn't even parked the coach. This caused a massive scramble on our coach to get off as soon as we had parked.

As soon as we were off the coach we ran up the hill leading to the ground, shattered by the time we reached the top. I could hear the noise from inside the stadium as we went through the turnstiles and we quickly ran up the approach and to our seats. Two minutes had been played of the match, but we were finally here!

Schalke started brightly testing Joe Hart twice through Jermain Jones but that was not going to stop the mighty blues. Sturridge raced down the left and crossed for Benjani to fire into the back of the net. Ireland then had a goal ruled out for offside before he finally beat Neuer to extend the lead to 0-2 to City. Cue pandemonium in the away end from the travelling blues.

The day in Köln was brilliant, the journey to Gelsenkirchen was very disappointing and we didn't even get a chance to look around the stadium. However the result was phenomenal considering even the most diehard of City fans were predicting a draw. We had finally arrived on the European stage (during my life time); through to the last 32 after a home win in the previous round of games.

The unrest from the Schalke fans was clear and as the clock ticked towards the 90 minute mark they started to file out of the stadium. It was the quietest it had been from the home fans all game, and as they trudged out the ground all you could hear were the City fans singing 'Schalke Auf Wiedersehen, Schalke Auf Wiedersehen'. **(Daniel Waldon)**

MANCHESTER CITY 0   PARIS SAINT-GERMAIN 0

UEFA Cup
Group Stage, Wednesday 3 December 2008
City of Manchester Stadium
Attendance: 25,326

PRESS VIEW

With City already sure of a last 32 place before kick-off, PSG ended the game pouring forward in search of a winner to leave them in a position where a victory at home to FC Twente on match day 5 would guarantee them qualification. However, the ball refused to fall for the Ligue 1 side, and they now need Mark Hughes's men to do them a favour at Real Racing Club if they are to move on. **(UEFA)**

City Team:
Hart, Zabaleta, Ben-Haim, Dunne, Garrido, Elano (Benjani), Vassell (Hamann), Kompany, Ireland, Jo (Evans), Sturridge
Subs: Schmeichel (GK), Logan, Berti, Caicedo

City, for all their initial pressure, were restricted to only half chances thereafter and, in the second half, PSG could have sealed victory but for a lack of composure in front of goal. The former Chelsea striker Mateja Kezman was a man possessed and fortunate not to have been dismissed following a series of reckless indiscretions. Having escaped with a warning for an elbow on Richard Dunne, Kezman produced a dangerous lunge on Joe Hart as the City goalkeeper cleared an under-hit back-pass from Sturridge and was finally cautioned for wrestling Tal Ben Haim to the floor. He also saw PSG's best chance of the first half blocked by a flying interception by the Israel defender. (*Guardian*)

The fans that stayed away had the right idea as this was not a game to live long in the memory. (*Sun*)

There was an eerie lack of tension and adrenalin in the freezing night air with some of the players dressed more for a Polar expedition than a game of football. (*Manchester Evening News*)

Snore Joke for Sparky
Manchester City boss Mark Hughes challenged his team to put their UEFA Cup group to bed, but instead they sent their fans to sleep with this bore draw against Paris St Germain. Victory for City would have sealed top spot in Group A. Hughes said "we had hoped to put the group to bed ahead of the game in Santander but we are at least guaranteed second place now. We have to remember that European football is a relatively new experience for us as a club though. European games can provide difficult tests for the players and PSG showed they have more experience of Europe than we do".

MANAGEMENT VIEW
We are guaranteed at least second and we are still in good shape. We are growing with every game we play in Europe. We want to avoid Champions League teams in the next stage. (**Kevin Keegan**)

REAL RACING CLUB 3   MANCHESTER CITY 1

Goal Scorer: Caicedo
UEFA Cup
Group Stage, Thursday 18 December 2008
Estadio el Sardinero, Santander, Spain
Attendance: 18,360

City Team:
Schmeichel, Zabaleta, Richards, Ben-Haim, Garrido, Vassell, Fernandes, Hamann, Elano, (Kompany), Robinho, (Ireland), Evans (Caicedo)
Subs: Hart (GK), Onuoha, Ball, Logan

PRESS VIEW
Manchester City suffered a crushing defeat at the hands of Racing Santander but still won Uefa Cup Group A because Paris St Germain beat FC Twente.

Santander took the lead after 18 minutes when Oscar Serrano's cross fell for Jonathan Pereira to tap home.

Serrano exchanged passes with Pereira to make it 2-0 on the half-hour mark and Juan Valera added a third after the break when a corner was not cleared. City were poor but replied with Felipe Caicedo's neat finish in injury time. (**BBC**)

Hughes will know that this might be the season of goodwill, but that does not extend to managers whose sides deliver duff displays like this. (*Sun*)

A dismal City display but they still win their group, while Santander crash out despite giving out a master class (*Daily Mirror*)

Hughes Headache as City slump

Manchester City somehow limped into the UEFA Cup draw as Group A winners despite a thumping first away defeat of the campaign that highlighted Mark Hughes' urgent need to reinforce his squad next month.

Granted Santander rose to the occasion of their biggest European tie with a magnificent performance that deserve to usher them into the draw. But substitute Felipe Caicedo's elegantly side footed goal, deep into time added on could not paper over City's cracks.

The manner of their dishevelled defeat, with stand in goal keeper Schmeichel at angry odds with his defenders over two of the goals, will hardly make the rest of Europe quake in their boots. The 1,000 fans who had trekked to Northern Spain had expected a better show at El Sardinero. City fell behind after 18 minutes and never looked likely to rescue things. Things took a turn for the worse on the half hour, when Serrano slipped through via a neat one-two with Pereira to pass the ball beyond Schmeichel. Juan Valera finally put City to the sword after 55 minutes and it could have been more with Mo Tchite missing an open goal.

MANAGEMENT VIEW

Ideally we would have preferred to have won the game, but credit to them, they are a good side. Their motivation was to try and get into the next round; we had already qualified so that might have taken a little bit of edge out of our game.

We have to take the positives out of it. We have topped the group and that was the order of the day. (**Mark Hughes**)

SUPPORTER'S QUOTE

'I have never seen anything as bad from City, long ball from the keeper; no one wants the ball, no confidence.' (**Bluebarra**)

FC COPENHAGEN 2   MANCHESTER CITY 2

Goal Scorers: Onuoha, Ireland
UEFA Cup
Round of 32 – First Leg, Thursday 19 February 2009
Parken Stadium, Copenhagen, Denmark
Attendance: 30,159

City Team: Given, Richards, Dunne, Onuoha, Bridge, Zabaleta, Kompany, Ireland, Wright-Phillips, Robinho (Caicedo), Bellamy
Subs: Hart (GK), Garrido, Weiss, Vassell, Elano

PRESS VIEW

FC Copenhagen managed to keep its UEFA Cup tournament hopes alive last night, netting an extra time goal from newly acquired Martin Vingaard to secure a 2-2. Although the home team played a solid match, the visitors controlled much of the play. (*Copenhagen Post*)

Manchester City hold the upper hand heading into their Uefa Cup clash with FC Copenhagen on Thursday. The Blues twice took the lead in the first leg of their last 32 encounter in Denmark, only to come away with a 2-2 draw.
However, two away goals could prove to be priceless as the tie heads to Eastland's. (**Sky Sports**)

Manchester City twice surrendered the lead as they drew with FC Copenhagen in their last-32 Uefa Cup first-leg tie. City were gifted the lead when keeper Jesper Christiansen shockingly allowed a tame Nedum Onuoha shot to squirm out of his grasp and into the net.
But Ailton Almeida punished some poor City marking by heading in a corner. Stephen Ireland's half-volley restored City's lead but Martin Vingaard was left free to head in an injury-time equaliser from Dame N'Doye's cross. (**BBC**)

City can be happy overall with two vital away goals in the Parken Stadium. But if they are to progress they need to be more clinical in front of goals. (***Sun***)

Manchester City came very close to proving fairy tales can come true in the land of Hans Christian Andersen. They were within two minutes of beating FC Copenhagen and now have a cracking chance of further progress in this competition
Two away goals ought to be enough to take care of a hard working Danes but the Blues will have to show the same kind of endeavour and a little more concentration when the two sides meet again. (***Manchester Evening News***)

Hughes boys get their act together on Euro Travels. (***Daily Mail***)

PLAYER & MANAGEMENT QUOTES

The lads turned in a very professional performance, especially when you take into account the conditions. I have been told the temperature dropped to minus during the match and the constant snow flurries also added to the testing conditions.

I think before the game we would have taken a positive result with away goals, but letting them get a goal back late is hard to take. **(Mark Hughes)**

We are obviously disappointed to lose a goal at that late stage because I thought we would see the game out quite comfortably at that point, but we have to look on the positive side, we got two away goals and overall put in a good, professional European performance. **(Mark Hughes)**

Only a bit of ball watching in injury time denied us a first leg win, but having scored two away goals, we are still in a very strong position to go through. **(Mike Summerbee)**

It was a game I expected us to do better in. I am not satisfied with the way we performed but it was our first game after the winter break and we made more mistakes than usual. **(Stale Solbakken, Copenhagen coach)**

SUPPORTERS' TALES - Tuborg! Carlsberg! Hvidtol! (Part 2)

Next on the tour of Denmark was Copenhagen in the last 32 of the competition, we were on the Thomas Cook trip and the weather was icy and snowy which made for treacherous conditions. We were dropped off in Tivoli gardens and made our way around the city. Copenhagen itself is an amazing place to visit, photo opportunities at nearly every corner. We found a bar 'Streckers' on one of the side streets and went in, ordered pints of Tuborg and sat down.

Upon going to the bar for a second time we were informed that if we showed our receipt from the previous round we would receive the contents of that receipt free. Brilliant! Buy one get one free on beer! A few other City fans that were in the pub had text their mates to inform them of the bargain on offer and within half an hour the place was flooded with City fans, flags and scarves.

The owners of the bar appeared and City fans mobbed them dressing them up in City colours and getting pictures with them. Another truly great European moment.

We left the bar and caught a train towards the Parken Stadium, getting off around ten minutes away. We walked the rest of the way to the stadium in the snowy conditions and past the lake that was completely frozen.

Finally we made it to the ground and had a look around although most of it was fenced off; we went into the stadium and waited for kick off. To our right the stand behind the goal was being done up so there was just a giant wall with a picture on it.

I had never seen anything like it so it was a little strange at first. As the teams came out the Copenhagen fans released a 2-tier length banner that had a lion on it (as

Copenhagen are nicknamed The Lions).

The game itself was a lively affair that finished 2-2, City went ahead as Nedum Onuoha raced forward and let fly a tame shot that somehow Jesper Christiansen allowed to squirm under his body and roll into the net, Ailton Almedia equalised for the hosts before Stephen Ireland restored the lead with a half volley. However on the 90th minute some slack defending allowed Copenhagen's Vingaard to head into the net and claim the equaliser, City however took 2 away goals back to the City Of Manchester Stadium. This game was memorable as we were penned into the top tier of the stadium by a mesh netting that one City fan took upon himself to climb up at every opportunity he had.

Whilst it was funny at the time and also entertaining when he climbed down you could see that the netting had cut his hands in several places and obviously he didn't try it after that!

After the game we made our way back to the Thomas Cook coaches to the airport, boarded the plane and I fell asleep. I woke an hour later thinking we were on our way back to Manchester. How wrong was I, we were still on the runway being de-iced by machines as the cold Danish weather had affected our plane. Finally we took off but the drama was only just starting, upon our approach to Manchester the plane circled for a good 30-40 minutes, the pilot claiming works on the runway were the cause. Rumours spread through the plane of a diversion to Birmingham Airport but then we started to descend, we touched down in Manchester a good hour later than expected and landed at the very end of the runway greeted by flashing lights that we just presumed were the workforce working on the runway.

The next day I received a text from someone on the plane saying that he had heard that the delay in landing in Manchester was not due to work on the runway but that the planes wheels were frozen into the plane and not coming out so we could land. We had apparently circled to lose fuel and we were going for an emergency landing when we descended into Manchester. The flashing lights had been fire engines and ambulances and we were at the end of the runway to cause the least amount of damage, however the wheels came finally came out and we made a smooth and controlled landing. Of course this was only rumour and whether or not it is true is another story. Another European trip over and optimism was fast spreading among the fans. (**Daniel Waldon**)

MANCHESTER CITY 2   FC COPENHAGEN 1

Goal Scorer: Bellamy (2)
UEFA Cup
Round of 32 – Second Leg, Thursday 26 February 2009
City of Manchester Stadium
Attendance: 26,018

City Team: Given, Richards, Onuoha, Dunne, Bridge, Zabaleta (Elano), Kompany, Wright-Phillips, Ireland, Robinho, Bellamy
Subs: Hart (GK), Vassell, Garrido, Caicedo, Berti, Evans

PRESS VIEW

Having struck the post just before half-time, Bellamy finally soothed nerves at Eastland's, seizing on a mistake from Copenhagen's 18-year-old centre-half, Mathias Jorgensen, as he tried to deal with a low, long up-field punt. He won the ball, turned sharply towards goal, and for someone whose finishing has been criticised throughout his career, scored sublimely. (*Guardian*)

Bellamy broke FC Copenhagen's resistance to secure a place in the last 16 of the UEFA Cup and a meeting with another Danish side in Aalborg.
   He scored twice in the space of seven second-half minutes to put this tie firmly to bed and leave City dreaming of further glory on the European stage. (*Sporting Life*)

City were the better side against limited opposition, indeed they proved themselves superior to Copenhagen over the two legs (*Daily Mail*)

It was just reward for another fine display and City reached the last 16 of a European competition for the first time in 30 years. (*Manchester Evening News*)

With two away goals from Denmark, City were in good shape to progress to the last 16 of the UEFA Cup. But, nevertheless, they needed to be on their toes because a Copenhagen victory would still have seen the visitors go through. (*Bluemoon*)

A tea-time downpour did not dampen the spirits of the visiting fans and their enthusiasm at kick-off ensured a good atmosphere inside the ground. The rain also ensured that the pitch was throwing up a bit of water as the ball travelled across the surface.
   But that was it and City had a thoroughly deserved win that could have been by a much wider margin. The Istanbul dream is still on. (**MCFC Website**)

MANAGEMENT VIEW

It was a strange night in some ways but after a slow start we raised the tempo and in fairness could have had more goals. We are delighted to be through, that was the order of the day and a lot of good sides have gone out surprisingly. (**Mark Hughes**)

MANCHESTER CITY 2   AALBORG BK 0

Goal Scorers: Caicedo, Wright-Phillips
UEFA Cup
Round of 16 – First Leg, Thursday 12 March 2009
City of Manchester Stadium
Attendance: 24,596

City Team: Given, Richards, Onuoha, Dunne, Bridge, Wright-Phillips (Etuhu), Zabaleta, Ireland, Elano, Robinho, Caicedo (Evans)
Subs: Hart (GK), Vassell, Garrido, Fernandes, Berti

PRESS VIEW

Manchester City took control of their Uefa Cup last-16 tie against Aalborg with a comfortable first-leg victory.

City took the lead after seven minutes when Felipe Caicedo muscled his way past Michael Jackobsen and fired home.

Caca forced a good save out of Shay Given as the Danes responded but Shaun Wright-Phillips made it 2-0 with a superb strike into the top corner. (**BBC**)

Fair Play entrants City have already knocked out FC Midtjylland and FC København in this season's competition and two neat finishes ensured a treble against Danish opposition is now a distinct possibility for England's only surviving UEFA Cup contenders. (**UEFA**)

Manchester's travel agents will be doing a roaring trade. United's imperious form has put them on the road to Rome. City, meanwhile, are patiently negotiating the byzantine structure of the Uefa Cup. They look destined for Istanbul.

Mark Hughes's side will surely find themselves in the pot for the quarter-finals a week today after goals from Felipe Caicedo and Shaun Wright-Phillips dispatched an AaB Aalborg side the hosts thoroughly outclassed.

The idea of Uefa Cup glory has clearly not captured the imagination of City's fans – Eastland's was scarcely half full – but with impressive home form and most of the competition's big names already fallen, they will have rarely had a better chance to end the club's 30-year wait for silverware. (***Daily Telegraph***)

The Blues showed the desire and concentration Hughes has been demanding from them and apart from a couple of scares they were always in control. (***Daily Mirror***)
The Danish outfit fought hard, but they're lucky to still have a sniff of a chance next Thursday. This result is surely good enough to City through to UEFA Cup quarter finals. (***Daily Star***)

Mark Hughes boys have a foot in the quarter finals. City may only need an away goal next Thursday to finish the job. (***Sun***)

Shaun stars as City take an early grip at Eastland's

Manchester City seized the upper hand in their UEFA Cup last-16 tie against Aalborg last night with a dominant first-leg display at Eastland's.

Inspired by England winger Shaun Wright-Phillips, Mark Hughes side were fast out of the blocks against their Danish opponents, and City, Britain's last remaining representative in the competition, went ahead on eight minutes when big Ecuadorian striker Felipe Caicedo collected Robinho's pass and shrugged off the challenge of Michael Jakobsen before firing past Karim Zaza.

The visitor's almost equalised when the skilful Caca stepped inside Nedum Onuoha before drilling in a shot that cannoned away off Shay Given's legs, but City settled any nerves when the excellent Wright-Phillips added a crucial second, driving home from the edge of the box on the half hour. City again threatened after the break with substitute Ched Evans impressing, but it was the Danes who ended on top with Kasper Risgard blazing over a free kick and Brazilian Caca slicing wide after incisive build up play.

MANAGEMENT & PLAYER QUOTES

The players are starting to sense we can win this now. We have to make sure we can get through but we're in good shape.

Once you start to get to quarter finals or semi-finals you get a real sense that you can do something great. But we're certainly enjoying the European experience. (**Mark Hughes**)

I'd like to think it was up there as one of my best goals for City. I just cut inside and let loose. (**Shaun Wright-Phillips**)

AALBORG BK 2   MANCHESTER CITY 0

City won 4-3 on penalties
UEFA Cup
Round of 16 – Second Leg, Thursday 19 March 2009
Energi Nord Arena, Aalborg, Denmark
Attendance: 10,735

City Team: Given, Richards, Dunne, Onuoha, Bridge (Garrido), Wright-Phillips, Zabaleta, Kompany (Elano), Ireland, Robinho, (Caicedo), Evans
Subs: Hart (GK), Fernandes, Etuhu, Berti

PRESS VIEW

City had been warned by manager Hughes they could not afford to concede an early goal with a lapse of concentration, and there was an air of anticipation in the EnergiNord Stadium on a chilly night as the Danes prepared to try to overturn their two-goal deficit from a fruitless trip to Manchester.

Aalborg fans indulged themselves in a flag-waving display as they awaited their team's assault on the Blues, while City's fans had a traditional inflatable banana to brandish back across the pitch, Hughes having already declared himself and his players proud to be flying the Union flag as Britain's last men standing in the UEFA Cup. (**MCFC Website**)

Manchester City won 4-3 on penalties to beat Aalborg and book their spot in the quarter-finals of the Uefa Cup. Goalkeeper Shay Given was City's hero as he saved from Thomas Augustinussen and Luton Shelton in the shoot-out.

Shelton had lashed in an 84th-minute shot just after a Robinho strike had hit the crossbar at the other end to give Aalborg hope of a comeback.

Michael Jakobsen powered in a penalty after a Ched Evans handball to level the tie 2-2 before City's dramatic win. (**BBC**)

The win kept alive City's hopes, as the last remaining English side in the event, of winning a first major piece of silverware since 1976.

Yet, on a bitterly cold night at the Energi Nord Arena, City were almost made to pay for their failure to kill off a tie they had dominated.

Shay Given saved two penalties as Manchester City snatched a place in the UEFA Cup quarter-finals despite a dramatic late collapse in Aalborg.

Protecting a 2-0 lead from the first leg, City were five minutes from progressing in normal time when the Danes staged a late fight back and took the game to extra-time thanks to goals from Luton Shelton and Michael Jakobsen.

It was left to Given to spare City's blushes and he delivered by keeping out spot-kicks from Thomas Augustinussen and former Sheffield United forward Shelton.

It was the second time in the Competition City had been taken to penalties by Danish opposition after a dramatic win over Midtjylland in the second qualifying round in August. (*Sporting Life*)

Another night of drama in Denmark and another nerve racking win on penalties for Manchester City as Shay Givens heroics sent them into the quarter finals of the UEFA Cup.

Last night they somehow contrived to give up a two goal advantage from the first leg in Manchester and a position of almost complete comfort, but then again nothing is ever comfortable with City. (*Daily Mail*)

City booked their first European quarter final place since 1979 but not before making their fans sweat buckets in the freezing cold of Aalborg. Any more of this and City really will believe that their names is etched on the silverware. (*Manchester Evening News*)

Who'd be a City Fan?

Trust Manchester to do their best to snatch defeat from the jaws of victory. Just when it seemed this game would peter out in a no-score bore, they reached for their well-worn self-destruct button to let loose all manner of mayhem. They conceded twice in the last five minutes to send the tie into extra-time and a nerve-shredding penalty shoot-out. Luckily for City, Shay Given kept his head when all about him were losing theirs to save two spot kicks and rescue them from disaster.

Early on there had been no sign of the late dramatics to come as Aalborg showed a distinct lack of ambition. Still there was no hint of a shock until five minutes from time when Shelton, controlled the ball and fired past Given. Then in the final minutes, Evans was harshly adjudged to have handled and Michael Jakobsen fired home the spot kick to level the tie on aggregate.

PLAYER & MANAGEMENT QUOTES

For 85 minutes, City were strolling into the quarter finals then out of nowhere were taken into extra time then a penalty shoot-out.

You start to think your name is on the trophy. It was maybe not the way we wanted to win but the dressing room is buzzing and maybe we can go on to win it now, who knows. **(Ched Evans)**

We dispatched our penalties with aplomb and showed great character but we should not have let it get that far. Over the two games we were the better team but there is that old adage that just when you think you are doing well the roof caves in and for five minutes that is exactly what happened. **(Mark Hughes)**

We made hard work of it. The game should have been dead and buried. We did not play our best but we are still in the draw. **(Shay Given)**

Knowing Shay was between the sticks, that gave us real confidence. The lads going up for penalties had a real belief that at some point Shay would play a hand. **(Mark Hughes)**

I'm disappointed because we put in a very good performance. If you look at the two games we deserved to go through. **(Magnus Pehrsson, Aalborg coach)**

SUPPORTERS' TALES

Dear Manchester City supporter

Thank you for your application for the official day trip package for the above game. For your information this trip has been oversubscribed. Unfortunately you have been unsuccessful on this occasion. Please accept our apologies for any disappointment caused that on this occasion we have been unable to accommodate you

Yours Sincerely
Thomas Cook Sport

So days before the game we get the above email, and panic mode sets in, with no tickets in hand as the Thomas Cook trip supplies you with them (subject to criteria), the keys on my laptop take a severe hammering as alternative ticket/travel arrangements were sort, fortunately an email from 'Flight Options' saves the day and there day trip promises the following. 'Depart Manchester Early morning for the short flight to Aalborg, arriving well in time for lunch. Sample the delights of the famous Jomfru Ane Gade, a street packed with bars and restaurants.'

All sounds good but somebody should have told the coach driver at the airport because he preceded to take us straight to the ground, what he expected us to do for the next few hours I have no idea, but he was soon persuaded to turn around. Most of the City travelling support of around 650 were present on the aforementioned avenue. So we decided to move slightly away and what a good decision it was after a couple of pints in a local Irish bar our next one was on the house as some City dignatries walked in and bought all the City fans in the bar a drink, something apparently they did in a few other bars.

As for the game City threw away a two goal cushion, and only progressed courtesy of a heart stopping penalty shoot out. **(Daniel John Thomas)**

Tuborg! Carlsberg! Hvidtol! (Part 3)

The final assault on Denmark was a last 16 tie against Aalborg, City held a healthy 2-0 home lead over the Danes and spirits were high that we would progress to the next round of the competition and make it a hat trick of wins against Danish Opposition.

Yet again we opted to join the Thomas Cook day trip, we flew out early morning into Aalborg and the coaches picked us up quickly and took us to the stadium to show us where we would be supporting the team later on in the day. The coaches then took us to the centre of the town and we were allowed to explore at our will. We went down to the waterfront to watch the bridges in operation for the passing ships and boats. As in all European tours to that date we found an Irish bar that welcomed City fans and sat down for a drink or two with some friends, an hour or so into our drinks two familiar faces walked into the pub that was slightly quiet and started chatting to us. Here we were in a pub in Aalborg and City legend Mike Summerbee and then chief executive Garry Cook had just walked in and started talking to us as if we were close friends. They bought us a round of drinks and mingled among the fans, before leading the group in a boisterous rendition of Bluemoon! The one thing we noticed was how much they seemed to love City and everything to do with the club. We finished our drinks and headed to a pub across the road that had some Aalborg fans in it, we got chatting and they produced a newspaper report from England that was an interview with Mark Hughes praising the team's spirit and hailing our first leg victory. The Danes took this the wrong way and presumed Mark Hughes was having a go at the Aalborg players and team, writing them off. No matter what we did to convince them they had got it wrong, we just couldn't break the language barrier and Mark Hughes had lost some more fans! Within our conversation with the Aalborg fans we asked them for predictions on the game, they were all confident they would win and knock us out. We protested and insisted that we would score from open play, the fact is we didn't.

The match started with the players in the tunnel and the Aalborg fans waving coloured flags along to the song 'Geordie' by Gabre Ponte, a techno rave sort of song that got all the fans bouncing and created a fantastic atmosphere. The game was a dull affair until the 85th minute; City had contained the host, and former Sheffield United striker Luton Shelton, well. Shelton controlled a cross well before firing past Shay Given. This gave the hosts a new lease of life as they raided forward in search of the goal that would send the tie to extra time, and it came.

A handball from Ched Evans in the 90th minute gave the hosts a penalty which Jakobson converted to send the game into extra time. Extra time passed without any incident and yet again City had a penalty shootout in Denmark to overcome, this time Shay Given was in net but the outcome was still the same. It was at the same end as the away fans and Aalborg failed to convert two of their penalties, Given saving both the penalties down to his right, the last from Luton Shelton, winning City the game and allowing them to progress into the last 8 of the competition.

City came away unscathed in the three games in Denmark and allowed us to continue our adventures with City over land and sea. **(Daniel Waldon)**

HAMBURG SV 3   MANCHESTER CITY 1

Goal Scorer: Ireland
UEFA Cup
Quarter Final – First Leg, Thursday 9 April 2009
HSH Nordbank Arena, Germany
Attendance: 50,500

City Team: Given, Richards, Dunne, Onuoha, Bridge (Garrido), Wright-Phillips (Fernandes), Zabaleta, Ireland, Sturridge (Benjani), Bellamy, Robinho
Subs: Hart (GK), Elano, Petrov, Berti

PLAYER & MANAGEMENT QUOTES
Hamburg are a good side, they have had an outstanding season and we can see the reasons why. We just have to pick ourselves up. We certainly do not think the tie is over. **(Mark Hughes)**

I would have preferred it if we had got another goal. We know it will be difficult if they score first next week but overall I am very happy. (**Martin Jol, Hamburg coach**)

The sell-out crowd was treated to a feast of attacking football. (**Hamburg Website**)

I have always been an optimist and this UEFA tie is not over yet. Hamburg are a good side and they have a 3-1 lead but we are not out of it by any means. (**Mike Summerbee**)

We are gutted because we had a great start but we were not brave enough after that and we have thrown it away. We only have ourselves to blame. (**Stephen Ireland**)

PRESS VIEW

Manchester City manager Mark Hughes saw his side make a stunning start in the UEFA Cup quarter-final then suddenly implode at the Nordbank Arena.

Stephen Ireland's opener after only 35 seconds only prompted an onslaught from Hamburg, who will take a two-goal cushion into the return leg at Eastland's next week.

City's hopes of progress are hanging by a thread after another dismal away day despite a superb display by goalkeeper Shay Given. (*Sporting Life*)

Hamburg really turned the screw in the second-half and City have an uphill struggle to stay in the competition at Eastland's. That away goal is all important though and may, just may, give them the glimmer of hope they will need. (**Guardian**)

Manchester City were emphatically beaten by Hamburg in the first leg of their quarter-final to leave their Uefa Cup hopes hanging by a thread.

The home side would have been in an even stronger position had it not been for City keeper Shay Given's heroics as the visitors' defensive frailties away from home were again exposed. (**BBC**)

Such are the fine margins in European football that a decent result can become a rather poor one in an instant and so it was in North Germany last night as a late goal from the shin of a Hamburg substitute left Manchester City with everything to do. (*Daily Mail*)

Hamburg was home to the Beatles in the early 1960s and it looks like Hello, Goodbye to Manchester City's Euro dream. (*Daily Mirror*)

Shay Givens goalkeeping heroics gave Manchester City the slimmest of chances of reaching the UEFA Cup semi-finals after they imploded in spectacular style. City's hopes of progress are hanging by a thread after another dismal away day. (*Daily Star*)

City fell apart under considerable pressure from the German side. They will need another electric start in the second leg at Eastland's to turn this tie around. *(Sun)*

City stunned by Jol's men

Such are the fine margins in European football that a decent result can become a rather poor one in an instant and so it was in North Germany last night as a late goal from the shin of a Hamburg substitute left Manchester City with everything to do at Eastland's next week.

Trailing 2-1 after Martin Jol's Hamburg had recovered from the shock of Stephen Ireland's first minute goal, City were in a decent shape with 11 minutes left. An away goal was at that point looking priceless but were unable to hold out and in the second period City's threat vanished and they were over-run at times, Joris Mathijsen escaped the attention of Nedum Onuoha to head across goal, Given got a hand to the ball but it crept in at the far post and then Trochowski nudged the home team ahead from the penalty spot in the 64th minute and the next 25 minutes were always going to be crucial and City could not manage to see the game out as they conceded an important third, Jose Paolo Guerrero converted high into the net. It was a victory Hamburg thoroughly deserved.

MANCHESTER CITY 2   HAMBURG SV 1

Goal Scorers: Elano (P), Caicedo
UEFA Cup
Quarter Final – Second Leg, Thursday 9 April 2009
City of Manchester Stadium
Attendance: 47,009

City Team: Given, Richards, Onuoha, Dunne, Bridge, Zabaleta (Fernandes), Kompany, Ireland, Elano (Sturridge), Robinho, Caicedo
Subs: Hart (GK), Garrido, Petrov, Evans, Logan

PRESS VIEW

City had a huge task to overturn a 3-1 first leg deficit but gave it a real go to push the Germans all the way. Down and out after a surrender in Hamburg, City came back to produce a performance packed with passion and vibrancy. *(Sun)*

Manchester City won a pulsating Uefa Cup quarter-final second leg against Hamburg but crashed out of the competition 4-3 on aggregate.

Hamburg took an early lead when Paolo Guerrero beat Shay Given from 12 yards.

Elano equalised from the spot for City, while the Brazilian twice hit the woodwork with brilliant free-kicks.

Felipe Caicedo, who later missed from close range, put City in front with a neat finish before Richard Dunne was sent off as Hamburg held on. **(BBC)**

Manchester City's hopes of ending their 33-year wait for a trophy were extinguished here on a night when they played with equal measures of spirit and togetherness but ultimately paid a heavy price for giving their Opposition too much of a head start. This was a courageous effort from Mark Hughes's team, toying with the crowd's nerves and emotions and coming agonisingly close to completing an improbable escape. (*Guardian*)

This was a glorious defeat for a team clearly determined to do their manager proud after so many dodgy displays in the past few months. (*Daily Mirror*)

PLAYER & MANAGEMENT QUOTES

We have to show that spirit every week. The fans gave us a massive lift. (**Stephen Ireland**)

City signed two of our best players in Vincent Kompany and Nigel De Jong, but I still think we were better over two legs. (**Martin Jol, Hamburg Coach**)

We took the game to them and on another night some of the chances we created fly in and we win the tie. But it was a great effort by everyone. Nobody gave us any chance to get anywhere near turning it around but we came very close. I thought the atmosphere was unbelievable, it was cracking right from the off. The supporters gave their all and we gave are all. (**Mark Hughes**)

2010-11 EUROPA LEAGUE

EB STREYMUR 0   MANCHESTER CITY 2

Goal Scorers: Petrov, Hamann
UEFA Cup
First Qualifying Round – First Leg, Thursday 17 July 2008
Faroe Islands National Stadium
Attendance: 5,400

City Team: Hart, Onuoha, Dunne, Richards, Ball, Ireland, Hamann (Gelson 74), Johnson, Petrov, Vassell, Jo (Evans 74)
Subs: Schmeichel, Corluka, Elano, Benjani, Castillo

PRESS VIEW

Mark Hughes got his Manchester City reign off to a winning start in the unlikely surroundings of the Faroe Islands

In truth, City were rarely troubled by the part-timers, despite a commendable effort from the Faroe league leaders

First-half goals from Martin Petrov and Dietmar Hamann gave City a comfortable, competent victory in this UEFA Cup first qualifying round first leg, seemingly making the second leg at Barnsley on July 31 a formality. (*Sporting Life*)

Mark Hughes' reign as Manchester City manager began with a comfortable win against EB Streymur in the first leg of the Uefa Cup first qualifying round.

The part-time Faroe Islanders never looked like causing a shock, although they did improve in the second half.

Martin Petrov's howitzer of a shot gave City an early lead, which they doubled before the break thanks to a spectacular Dietmar Hamann volley. (**BBC**)

The contest was all over after 28 minutes on a pitch dug into a hillside overlooking the capital Torshavn. (*Daily Mirror*)

I was pleased with the performance, particularly in the first half when we kept possession well.

It could have been more comprehensive but two goals away from home in Europe and a clean sheet is a good result. (**Mark Hughes**)

Even what appeared a simple trip to the Faroe Island to swot away the challenge of an amateur side in this qualifying round did not slip through the British sporting summer without attracting more than its fair share of attention.

The national stadium was almost full, with the crowd of 5,400 including 250 hardy souls from Manchester, including 12 who arrived via ferry - but only as far as the Shetlands. The final leg should have been by hired trawler, but rough weather scuppered that plan and the Faroes airline, Atlantic, stepped in with free flights to the match.

An impressed Hughes made a point of welcoming them to the Torsvollur stadium beforehand.

It was not perhaps a classic performance they witnessed, as the game had an air of pre-season about it, but City were effective and did the job they came to do.

Petrov's show gets Hughes off mark

Mark Hughes began his Manchester City reign with a win in the Faroe Islands, but his new team looked far from slick against an amateur outfit. Martin Petrov and Dietmar Hamann had City in front inside half an hour, but that was all they could manage.

With 5,400 fans crammed into the Torsvallur stadium, City were given a scary couple of early moments against the feisty amateurs, but City soon showed their superiority and took the lead when Petrov planted a powerful shot into the top corner after Michael Johnson had cleverly stepped over Vassell's pass and when Streymur failed to clear a corner from Petrov, Hamann doubled the lead prodding a neat volley past Torgard from just outside the box.

MANCHESTER CITY 2   EB STREYMUR 0

Goal Scorers: Petrov, Vassell

UEFA Cup

First Qualifying Round – Second Leg, Thursday 31 July 2008

Oakwell Stadium, Barnsley

Attendance: 7,344

With the Eastland's pitch having to be re-laid following the recent pop concert the return game in the UEFA cup against EB Streymur had to be played at the Oakwell ground in Barnsley so the 'home' supporters were given a free coach ride from COMS to Barnsley.

City Team: Hart, Corluka, Dunne, Richards, Ball, Gelson (Hamann 62), Johnson, Elano, Petrov (Etuhu 69), Vassell, Sturridge (Evans 70)
Subs: Schmeichel, Onuoha, Ireland, Bianchi

PRESS VIEW

The game was played at Oakwell, the home of Championship side Barnsley, as the pitch at Eastland's is not yet ready after being re-laid in the close season.

But unusual surroundings or not, City created a glut of chances from the very start and the scoreline does not reflect the totally one-sided nature of the game.

Manchester City won their Uefa Cup first qualifying-round tie after a comfortable second-leg victory over EB Streymur of the Faroe Islands.

City dominated from the off, with Streymur's Rene Torgard making a string of saves while Vedran Corluka and Martin Petrov hit the woodwork.
Petrov volleyed into an empty net from Darius Vassell's cross for the first goal as City won 4-0 on aggregate.

Vassell scored late on from a tight angle after rounding the keeper. **(BBC)**

Thanks Pet-It's a Faroe struggle for Sparky Boys

Martin Petrov and Darius Vassell saw City through their UEFA Cup opener, but they hardly won in a blaze of Glory. Last month's Bon Jovi concert meant the Eastland's pitch was not ready and forced the tie to be switched to Barnsley. As a result Mark Hughes first 'home' game as boss was low key with the spirited Faroe Islands part timers refusing to lie down.

There was never any doubt Sparky's boys would be in the second qualifying round draw following a 2-0 lead from the first leg. But the 7,000 City fans who trekked across the Pennines must have hoped for more goals as keeper-cum-mechanic Rene Torgard made their side sweat. Torgard twice denied playmaker Elano with excellent saves. Vedran Corluka also thumped a header against the bar and Petrov fizzed a low shot against a post before City made the break through just after half time. Vassell did well down the right and his cross found the unmarked Petrov to side foot home.

The Bulgarian could have doubled his tally when he raced onto Did Hamann's through-ball and beat Torgard with a chip, but saw his effort also clear the bar. City had a seemingly endless string of chances but could not add to their tally. Finally in stoppage time, sub Ched Evans flick sent Vassell clear to round Torgard before scoring.

MANAGEMENT VIEW

They defended extremely well. It was damage limitation from them really, but you have to give them praise for their efforts.

Their goalkeeper had a wonderful night; they threw bodies in the way of everything and made life very difficult for us.

I was pleased with my lads. They kept at them and if their goalkeeper had not had such a great night, we would have won it at a canter. (**Mark Hughes**)

FC TIMISOARA 0 MANCHESTER CITY 1

Goal Scorer: Balotelli
UEFA Europa League
Play Off – First Leg, Thursday 19 August 2010
Stadionul Dan Paltinisanu
Attendance: 20,000 to 28,000

City Team: Hart, Zabaleta, K. Toure, Kompany, Lescott, Y. Toure, De Jong, Barry (Balotelli), Tevez (Jo), Adebayor, Silva (A. Johnson)
Subs: Given (GK), Richards, Vieira, Wright-Phillips

Manchester City's £24m striker Mario Balotelli came off the bench to score on his debut as they won their Europa League play-off first leg in Timisoara.

Balotelli came on with City struggling against the little-known Romanians and with 18 minutes left he coolly fired in after good work from Emmanuel Adebayor.

Timisoara had started well and had two penalty appeals turned down as City laboured for long periods. But soon after Yaya Toure hit the post, Balotelli grabbed the decisive goal.

PRESS VIEW

Roberto Mancini's team were treading water, lethargic and uninspiring prior to Balotelli's 56th minute introduction as a replacement for Gareth Barry.

Yet once the former Inter Milan forward, described as 'unmanageable' by Mourinho, had entered the fray, Mancini's team was transformed and provided the potency they had so painfully lacked without him. (***Daily Telegraph***)

It was all so dull in a game that had been billed as the 'Game of the Decade' by the local media, until Mario Balotelli arrived to grab the headlines, not for the last time. (***Sun***)

The home side were promised a £82,000 win bonus and did their best to bag the money. Timisoara threw everything at City but the away side at least looked solid at the back under an unexpected assault from the underdogs. (***Daily Star***)

SUPPORTERS' TALES – Poli's Poppy Seeds

The 2010/11 Europa League season kicked off with City facing Romanians FC Timisoara at the Dan Paltinisanu Stadium. To get to Romania we decided it would be best to make our own way there so a flight into Munich and an overnight stay at the NH Munich airport hotel were a pit stop on our way to Timisoara. After spending a day and night in Munich we arrived back at the airport ready to depart on our trip to Romania. The flight was called and we made our way to the shuttle bus to the plane. We passed many chartered planes on the runway each one a jumbo jet or the standard Boeing 737. Looking around at the number of people on the shuttle bus we presumed none of these were for us, we were right. At the end of the runway was a small propeller run aircraft, seating no more than forty people, operated by 'Carpet Air'. We clambered aboard the aircraft and could literally see the back of the plane in detail from our seats at the front. The stewardess came through the cabin offering a paper, all in Romanian, we took one anyway to see if there was anything on City (there wasn't). We arrived in Timisoara around an hour or so later and got picked up by the hotel we were staying at. The hotel was a stone's throw away from the ground and we had a balcony that we could observe the stadium from.

As the countdown to the game got closer to kick off the streets around the stadium started to fill with food vendors. However, this was not our normal burger and chips van. They were selling poppy seeds, sunflower seeds. All type of seeds!

We decided to leave the hotel and have a look around the town. We found a nice square and got some food from a restaurant there. We couldn't believe how cheap it was, 3 course meal and drinks for 2 was around £10 and the food was not bad either. We then took a seat in a bars forecourt and had a beer called Silva Bullet simply because of the name of it!

We then made our way back to the stadium for the game. For this match we were not sitting with the City fans. The hotel we were staying at got us tickets for hospitality seating. We looked at the stalls that had popped up selling Timisoara merchandise and visited the small club shop too; we then made our way into the ground to take up our seating.

The game had a good tempo to it but City couldn't break down a solid Timisoara side that had clearly upped their game in front of their adoring fans. Waving them on with large flags and a well organised ultras group behind the goal to our right they gave City a good battle.

However the game would eventually be City's for the taking. Mario Balotelli coming on as a substitute, in his first appearance for us, scored the only goal of the game before getting injured during injury time.

City won one nil taking back the win and the important away goal back to the City of Manchester stadium. Timisoara away was a brilliant European experience for me as the Romanian culture is so much different to that of our English culture and travelling Europe with City allows us to see our club on a greater stage. Another good win and a further step to announcing ourselves on the big stage. Job done. (**Daniel Waldon**)

MANCHESTER CITY 2   FC TIMISOARA 0

Goal Scorers: Wright-Phillips, Boyata
UEFA Europa League
Play Off – Second Leg, Thursday 26 August 2010
City of Manchester Stadium
Attendance: 23,542

City Team: Hart, Richards, Kompany, Boyata, Zabaleta, Wright-Phillips, De Jong (Cunningham), Vieira, Silva, Adebayor, Jo
Subs: Given (GK), Lescott, Y. Toure, Barry, Tevez, A. Johnson

Manchester City eased into the group stages of the Europa League with a comfortable win against FC Timisoara.

Shaun Wright-Phillips doubled the first-leg advantage with a low finish from eight yards after he was put through by Patrick Vieira.

Defender Dedryck Boyata made it 2-0 on the night with a close-range header from David Silva's corner.

In a match dominated by the English side, Silva, Emmanuel Adebayor and Jo also came close to scoring.

Romanian side Timisoara barely troubled City keeper Joe Hart. A first-half effort from Mircea Axente which hit the side-netting was the only cause of concern for Roberto Mancini's side.

Rob's boys have loads in reserve

Roberto Mancini saw his star spangled second stringers justify his massive summer buying spree. The most expensive reserve team in the game eased City into the Europa League group draw.

City piled on the pressure and it was merely a matter of time before Timisoara cracked under the strain and the moment arrived when De Jong slipped a square pass to Viera whose piercing through ball was clipped first time by Wright-Phillips into the bottom corner and Timisoara's fading hopes were crushed when Boyata headed in at the far post from Silva's right wing free kick in the 59th minute. Adebayor should have made it three two minutes later when Burca facing his goal, squared the ball to the City striker whose close range shot trickled wide of the far post.

MANAGEMENT VIEW

It is an important trophy. I think the Europa League is difficult because you play more games. But if we can change some players every game, I think we can arrive at the end and play in the final.

It is not like the Champions League, sure, but it is important.

We started the game very well, had a good focus. It was difficult because they had 10 players behind the ball and sometimes we couldn't find any space. But I think it was a good game. **(Roberto Mancini)**

FC RED BULL SALZBURG 0   MANCHESTER CITY 2

Goal Scorers: Silva, Jo
UEFA Europa League
Group Stage, Thursday 16 September 2010
Stadion Salzburg (Red Bull Arena)
Attendance: 25,100

City Team: Hart, Zabaleta, Kompany, K. Toure, Bridge (Boyata), Silva (Wright-Phillips), Y. Toure, De Jong, Barry, Tevez (Vieira), Jo
Subs: Given (GK), Richards, Milner, A. Johnson

David Silva scored his first goal for Manchester City to help them to victory over Red Bull Salzburg in their opening Europa League group match.

The Spanish World Cup winner side footed in the opener from eight yards following striker Jo's lay-off.

City doubled their lead after the break when Jo followed up Gerhard Tremmel's save from Carlos Tevez's 20-yarder.

Salzburg created few clear-cut chances, with their best falling to Ibrahim Sekagya, whose shot struck the bar.

PRESS VIEW

Jo-in classic centre-forward style – was first to react to slot home the rebound.

The goal effectively killed of the game, and the home team were visibly deflated. Sensing this, the English team regained control of the match. After sporadic pressure from the Austrians, City were quite happy to knock the ball around and soak up the remaining fight left in Salzburg.

In the end, it was a comfortable win for City in their opening group game and Roberto Mancini will be happy with his team's professionalism. Not a game for the purists perhaps, but the away fans will be pleased with Silva getting off the mark, and Jo making a scoring contribution as Emmanuel Adebayor's replacement. (*Goal*)

It was a job well done by City, whose hopes of getting near some silverware this season in Europe must now be soaring. (*Daily Mail*)

David Silva proved Red Bull does give you wings as his Manchester City career finally took flight in Salzburg. (*Daily Mirror*)

Silva just pure gold raves Rob

David Silva kicked his critics into touch here last night by giving Manchester City's hopes of European glory a massive boost. The attacking midfielder certainly went a long way towards silencing the doubters with a great goal scoring display in his teams opening Europa League Group A game.

Silva opened the scoring for City to help his side to three invaluable points in a competition in which they really look to have a chance of doing well. His overall performance was excellent and he showed that he can live up to the price tag on his shoulders following his move from Valencia. With City always in control against the Austrians, it was no surprise when they went further ahead in the 63rd minute when Jo powered home a rebound after a shot from Tevez was palmed away by keeper Gerhard Tremmel.

It was a job well done by City, whose hopes of getting near some silverware this season in Europe must now be soaring.

City hit all the right notes in the birthplace of Mozart and struck gold thanks to their two Silva's. (*Sun*)

MANAGEMENT QUOTES

Silva is a fantastic player - for him it is a different situation now.

He is playing a different kind of football. But after one month, he is ready to go 100 per cent for the team.

He will be an important player for the future. He is a strong player who played for Valencia in the Champions League for many years. (**Roberto Mancini**)

We did not start very well, and if you are not on top of your game in the first 10 minutes against a team such as Manchester City, it is always going to be a struggle.

We gave City too much space, and they had too much room to get at our defence. (**Huub Stevens, Salzburg coach**)

David showed what an amazing talent he is, but like every foreign player he needs time to settle. (**Vincent Kompany on Silva**)

MANCHESTER CITY 1   JUVENTUS 1

Goal Scorer: A. Johnson
UEFA Cup
Group Stages, Thursday 30 September 2010
City of Manchester Stadium
Attendance: 35,212

City Team: Hart, Zabaleta (Boyata), K. Toure, Kompany, Boateng (Milner), A. Johnson, Viera, Y. Toure, Barry, Tevez, Adebayor (Silva)
Subs: Given (GK), Lescott, Jo, De Jong

PRESS VIEW

Manchester City came from behind to secure a hard-fought draw with Juventus in an entertaining Europa League Group A encounter at Eastland's.

The Italian giants dominated the early stages and Vincenzo Iaquinta opened the scoring with a drive from distance. But City battled back and after Gareth Barry's header hit a post, Adam Johnson met Yaya Toure's pass to slot home. Barry shot over and Alessandro Del Piero hit a free-kick against the bar, but neither side could find a winner.

The result was probably a fair reflection of proceedings and it puts City level with Lech Poznan, who beat Salzburg 2-0 to move top of the group by virtue of goals scored, on four points. (**BBC**)

Struggling a little to juggle the demands of their European and domestic commitments. City fielded a strong team and it was just as well, given the manner in which they were required to scrap for what they achieved. (*Daily Mail*)

Roberto Mancini might have a soft spot for Juventus but he was left cursing his boyhood heroes at Eastland's. He probably did not know whether to laugh or cry at the outcome of this Europa League Group A Clash. (*Daily Star*)

Manchester City survived a late scare to collect a point from their high-profile Europa League clash with Juventus.

Roberto Mancini's men had run out of attacking ideas themselves when veteran forward Alessandro Del Piero strode up to blast a free-kick off the underside of Joe Hart's crossbar.

Del Piero claimed the ball bounced in, but the merits of a goal-line assistant were plain to see as the official correctly ruled it had come down straight onto the goal-line. (*Sporting Life*)

Adam Johnson's first European goal for Manchester City FC earned Roberto Mancini's side a point from their UEFA Europa League home meeting with Juventus.

Luigi Delneri's visitors took an early lead through Vincenzo Iaquinta's long-range effort but Johnson levelled eight minutes before the interval. City lacked the spark to open up the visitors a second time, though, and Juventus almost grabbed all three Group A points when Alessandro Del Piero's late free-kick hit the crossbar. (**UEFA**)

City so slick as Johnson learns fast

Adam Johnson's crucial goal against one of the most respected club sides in Europe did the job, when he scored what yet could prove to be a decisive one in the context of City's Europa League season.

City had fallen behind to a goal that rocked them on 10 minutes; a sweetly struck shot from distance by Vincenzo Iaquinta should have been saved by Joe Hart. Del Piero then struck the underside of the bar from distance it was turning out to be not a great night for the England keeper.

Juventus were dangerous when shooting from distance; City for their part struck the post from Gareth Barry before Johnson's goal brought them back into the game.

Manchester City have to rely on the imminent release of their financial results to make European football sit up and take notice after an obdurate Juventus denied the club a headline Europa League victory at Eastland's. Adam Johnson's first-half goal, which cancelled out Vincenzo Iaquinta's tenth minute opener, secured a 1-1 draw in this Group A encounter against Italy's fallen giants. (*Daily Telegraph*)

A draw was always likely with two Italians in the dugouts. But Juve came so close to winning it at the end. (*Sun*)

MANAGEMENT VIEW

Adam is a good young player, but we would like him to improve. He scored a good goal and did something good, but at the same time, he can always improve.

We thought we could control the game, but after Laquinta scored, the match changed. But I am confident for the Europa League. It is a difficult group because Lech Poznan (City's next opponents) are a good team, but I still believe we can go through. **(Roberto Mancini)**

SUPPORTERS' VIEWS

'We did not get going until we scored but a draw is not a bad result against a good Juventus side.'

'Frustrated. I never thought I would be disappointed with City drawing with Juve but too many players were just slightly off their game.'

'That was a poor performance. I think we saw why we are being linked with so many forwards.'

'Kompany showed what a great defender he is becoming.'

MANCHESTER CITY 3 KKS LECH POZNAN 1

Goal Scorer: Adebayor (3)
UEFA Europa League
Group Stage, Thursday 21 October 2010
City of Manchester Stadium
Attendance: 33,383

City Team: Hart, Lescott, Richards, Boyata, Zabaleta (Bridge), De Jong, Vieira, Wright-Phillips (Jo), Silva (Y. Toure), A. Johnson, Adebayor
Subs: Given (GK), Kompany, Milner, Tevez

PRESS VIEW

Emmanuel Adebayor became the first Manchester City player to score a hat-trick in Europe in a win that puts them top of Europa League Group A.

Adebayor opened the scoring with a superb turn and finish from the edge of the area early in the first half.

The striker doubled the lead soon after with a header from David Silva's cross.

Joel Tshimbamba scored from close range to make it 2-1 but Adebayor neatly finished another Silva cross to end the Polish side's spirited challenge.

The result leaves City with seven points from three group stage games, three points clear of Lech.

Roared on by anywhere between a Fervent noise of 6,000 to 9,000 strong travelling support, the Polish side were not going to give in easily but they simply had no answer to Adebayor. (**Daily Express**)

Another entertaining night in the European competition thanks to Lech Poznan and their fans. Kolejorz played to the best of their abilities, but at the moment their abilities don't enable them to compete on equal terms with the likes of Manchester City. Still, they showed enough character in the second half to leave the faithful fans satisfied. (**Polish Web Blog**)

Feast-Lands joy for Ade

Emmanuel Adebayor blew away the cobwebs to resurrect his faltering Manchester City career; the former Arsenal striker grabbed a brilliant hat trick to help City cement their place at the top of Europa League Group A.

In his joy at exorcising his goal scoring demons, he celebrated each of them by brushing away imaginary cobwebs off his kit and he left the pitch with the match ball, first of all waving it to the crowd and then tucking it under his shirt for safe keeping.

City took the lead in the 13th minute, Patrick Vieira collected the ball from David Silva and slipped in a perfect pass into the path of Adebayor, with his back to goal, he turned and cool as you like pushed a right foot shot past keeper

Jasmin Buric. Silva produced a cracking left wing cross to set up City's second in the 25th minute of a game they dominated for lengthy spells. Adebayor eight yards out found himself with plenty of time and space to place a towering header into the back of the net.

Poznan pulled a goal back, when Zabaleta made a hash of clearing the ball and Marchin Kikut's shot was deflected into the path of Joel Tshibamba who scored from seven yards.

City then turned on the style and Adebayor completed his hat trick by rounding off a fine move in the 73rd minute. Shaun Wright-Phillips and Vieira combined well before Silva sent over a lovely looping low pass which Adebayor tapped in from a few yards.

PLAYER QUOTES

The Europa League is an important competition and an important trophy, and Manchester City cannot afford to be arrogant towards any cup or trophy because we have not won anything for a long time. **(Vincent Kompany)**

I'm very happy to become the first player to score a hat-trick for the club in Europe. **(Emmanuel Adebayor)**

KKS LECH POZNAN 3   MANCHESTER CITY 1

Goal Scorer: Adebayor
UEFA Europa League
Group Stage, Thursday 4 November 2010
Stadion Miejski
Attendance: 43,000

City Team Given, Zabaleta, Richards, Boyata, Lescott, A. Johnson, Vieira, Bridge (Kolarov), Wright-Phillips (Silva), Milner (Kompany), Adebayor
Subs: Hart (GK), Barry, Jo, Balotelli

City started well but it was hosts Lech who opened the scoring, Dimitrije Injac fizzing in a low strike from distance.

Emmanuel Adebayor's close-range finish pulled the visitors level and David Silva volleyed against the crossbar.

A draw seemed inevitable until Manuel Arboleda inadvertently nodded in and Mateusz Mozdzen rifled a fine third.

It ended the club's six-match unbeaten run in European competition, cost them top spot in the group and meant they squandered the chance to qualify for the knockout phase with two games to spare.

PRESS VIEW

The manner of City's defeat was that unfortunate. The side had demonstrated admirable fight in recovering from a goal down in a hostile environment. (***Daily Telegraph***)

If City were hoping to blame bad luck for their latest defeat, they were hit by an emphatic third goal in the 90th minute. The ball was played to Mateusz Mozdzen 30 yards out and Boyata was slow to close down the space as the Poznan midfielder let fly with a stunning drive that flew into the top corner.

It was a wonderful strike to cap a famous win for the Poles who deserved to celebrate in front of their supporters at the end. (***Daily Mail***)

Before the game even die hard Lech fans were only hoping for a draw. However, with a passionate display and lady luck on their side Kolejorz has managed to put in their best display since 2008. Now Lech has got a serious chance to advance to the play off stage and leave either Manchester City or Juventus behind.

What a night, what a result. Lech exceeded all expectations. (***Polish Soccer***)

A late collapse by Manchester City allowed Lech Poznan to collect a vital Europa League victory.

Roberto Mancini's men looked to have secured a valuable point after Emmanuel Adebayor had cancelled out Dimitrije Injac's opener early in the second half.

But goals by Manuel Arboleda and Mateusz Mozdzen late on mean City will have to collect maximum points against Salzburg to guarantee their place in the last 32. (***Daily Record***)

MANAGEMENT VIEW

I'm disappointed to lose the game but we were missing 10 players who were at home. We played a good game but we were unlucky.

We didn't deserve to lose the game. Everything is against us. We are very unlucky but that's football.

This game was very strange. If we played it 100 times we would win 90 of them. Sometimes the club with the money does not win.

We are still in the Europa League and fourth in the Premier League. It's a difficult situation and we must change it, but we can only change things if we stay together. **(Roberto Mancini)**

SUPPORTERS' VIEWS

'Pressure is absolutely useless unless you can hit the onion bag.'

'Again, not brilliant, but Mancini was hampered in his selection.'

'Oh dear, the second string is not good enough.'

'Some of the players need to take a good look at themselves after yet another poor performance.'

'Another poor defensive display and again nobody up front to put the ball in the net.'

Let's all do the Poznan

When City were drawn against Lech Poznan in Group A of the Europa League season 2010/11 it was seen as a blessing in disguise in our household. My Dads Partner is of Polish decent and most of her relatives came from Poznan so it was a win all round as it meant we could go away for football whilst visiting relatives at the same time.

We flew out from Liverpool's John Lennon airport straight in Poznan and were greeted by family members who took us to our hotel. We checked in and left immediately to see some more extended family, the hospitality shown was fantastic and I got a real taste of what it was like to live in Poznan and how the locals went about their day to day lives. We were taken on a tour of Poznan and its city as well as some of the outskirts too. This included an amazing experience in the old square watching the two goats in the clock tower come out to greet each other at midday. This attracted a huge crowd every day and it was an amazing feat to see such great history in action.

To say we jumped feet first into Polish culture is an understatement as I was literally a local by the end of the first day. Sampling the local cuisine as well as learning the local language as well as visiting extended family in hospital whilst effectively being a baby sitter too!

The food too was a revelation, I had these amazing bread style dumplings that were used as an alternative to potatoes and I must admit they were one of the nicest things I had ever tried and have subsequently found them in the Arndale indoor market in Manchester City Centre.

The trip to Poznan is probably the best of all the European trips I have done as we were made to feel welcome from the offset. We had a spare ticket for the game and were not going to do anything with it; this was until we had lunch at a relative's house the day of the game. Whilst waiting for dessert to be served one of the extended family members put on a CD. It was a CD based fully on Manchester City, a CD that he had burned himself in anticipation of our arrival. We duly offered him the ticket as a good will gesture. He obliged.

So there we were, we had been driven to the ground and parked up. Explored Lech's amazing new stadium built for the European championships in 2012 and was now sat in the away end, amongst all the City fans, with one boisterous Pole. Keep his head down and all will be okay I thought.

The game kicked off and Lech started their attack. He could barely contain his excitement letting out gasps and cheers as the Poles applied the pressure. A few glances from fellow City fans was enough for us to tell him to calm down, after all he was just a friendly Polish man enjoying a football game between his local team and Manchester City.

Lech scored first and the stadium erupted into noise I had barely heard at any other stadium before, it was loud. Very loud.

One thing that fascinated me whilst we were there was a section amongst the home fans that was fenced off, turns out it was for Wisla Krakow fans that turn up nearly every game to cheer on Lech. I also noted a huge banner in the Ultras end of the ground from the team Arka Gdynia. Yet again this was strange to me as you wouldn't see a West Brom banner in the midst of the Kop at Anfield just before a game. These banners signified a footballing brotherhood between the fans of these teams. Strange.

Back to the game and City equalized through Emanuel Adebayor. The game was evenly poised and heading for a draw until Manuel Arboleda unknowingly headed the ball into the net after Boyata cleared a cross onto his head in the 86th minute.

Lech had their tails up and went in search for another that finally came in the 91st minute when substitute Mateusz Mozdzen fired in an unstoppable shot from far out that beat Joe Hart. The result was confirmed and the Poznan fans celebrated like there was no tomorrow. Their victory was well deserved as City never really got going.

In the car on the way back there were two very sullen faces and one gleaming from ear to ear. It doesn't take a rocket scientist to work out who that happy one was, he had enjoyed his first European game and we weren't about to ruin it for him. After all City were going home with their tails between their legs after a comprehensive score line that didn't really flatter the home team. Underdogs? **(Daniel Waldon)**

MANCHESTER CITY 3   FC SALZBURG 0

Goal Scorers: Balotelli (2), A. Johnson
UEFA Europa League
Group Stage, Wednesday 1 December 2010
City of Manchester Stadium
Attendance: 37,552

City Team: Given, Boateng, K. Toure (Richards), Lescott, Zabaleta, Wright-Phillips, Milner, Vieira, A. Johnson, Balotelli (Adebayor), Jo
Subs: Hart (GK), Kolarov, Barry, Silva, De Jong

PRESS VIEW

Mario Balotelli scored twice to help Manchester City to victory over Salzburg that takes them into the last 32 of the Europa League.

The Italian striker opened the scoring with a hooked volley from Pablo Zabaleta's left-wing cross.

He added a second after the break when he tapped in Patrick Vieira's mis-hit shot which had fallen at his feet.

And Adam Johnson added City's third late on when he weaved past three players before slotting in. **(BBC)**

Balotelli turned up the heat on a freezing night with goals in each half to sink Salzburg. **(*Daily Star*)**

Mario Balotelli gives City wings, as Red Bull Salzburg found out to their cost. The Italian is a class act and was the difference here. (*Sun*)

The City fans celebrated in the snow last night and sang songs in jest about Salzburg's Brazilian striker Alan, but are hardly going to miss him when they have someone like Balotelli. (*Daily Mail*)

Balotelli was as chilled as the weather to slot home his goals and he brought a little ray of sunshine to sub-zero Manchester to fire City into the knockout stage of the Europa League. (*Manchester Evening News*)

Tellis a real turn on

Mario Balotelli fired Manchester City into the Europa League knockout stages with a double strike at Eastland's, but it still was not enough to earn the praise of tough task master Roberto Mancini.

Balotelli turned up the heat on a freezing night with goals in each half to sink Salzburg. He pounced on 18 minutes with a smart volley before adding a second just after the hour. Adam Johnson also weighed in with a stunning solo effort on 77 minutes, with a weaving run past four defenders that ended with a curling strike into the bottom corner to book City's passage from Group A with a game to spare.

The Austrian outfit never looked like scoring to leave Shay Given in danger of catching frostbite.

MANAGEMENT VIEW

I'm happy with qualification - we can now focus on the Premier League.

We could have had a better result had we converted our three or four chances in the first half. (**Roberto Mancini**)

He's a good striker but he must improve. He can play better than he did tonight. (**Roberto Mancini on Balotelli**)

He scored a good goal tonight and I'm happy for him because he's a good guy. But like Mario, he can play better. (**Roberto Mancini on Johnson**)

JUVENTUS 1   MANCHESTER CITY 1

Goal Scorer: Jo
UEFA Europa League
Group Stage, Thursday 16 December 2010
Stadio Olimpico, Turin
Attendance: 6,992

City Team: Given, Richards, Boyata, Boateng, Bridge, Wright-Phillips (Chantler), Milner, Vieira, A. Johnson, Jo, Nimely (Zabaleta)
Subs: Taylor (GK), Kay, Mee, Ibrahim, Elabdellaoui

PRESS VIEW

A neat finish by Jo earned Manchester City a point away to Juventus and ensured they advanced to the Europa League last 32 as group winners.

At the end of a poor first half, Juve debutant Niccolo Giannetti nipped in front of Dedryck Boyata to score.

With Lech Poznan winning, City seemed set to finish second in the group and potentially face a tougher draw.

But after 76 minutes, Jo spun on a pass from the excellent Adam Johnson and slotted home a low shot from 12 yards.

Jo, one of only two players retained from the weekend win against West Ham, and Johnson will have been relatively happy with their night's work, but few others shone in a game that often had the feel of a not particularly taxing pre-season friendly. **(BBC)**

A makeshift City side secured top spot in their Europa League group by holding Juventus to a one-all draw at a sparsely populated Stadio Olimpico.

Although the travelling squad was trimmed of many star names, the game represented a chance for those on the fringe domestically to impress. **(MCFC WEB)**

It is probably a measure of how far Manchester City have come, and the new sense of ambition that comes from being bankrolled by some of the wealthiest men on earth, that they should regard a draw against Juventus one of the great names in European football, as cause for disappointment. *(Guardian)*

Manchester City secured top spot in Group A after coming from behind in their Europa League match to take a point against Juventus in Turin.

Jo, the only senior striker in the team, rose to the challenge to cancel out the opening goal from Niccolo Giannetti.

The Brazilian kept a cool head in the 77th minute to sweep the ball home at the back post following a cross from Adam Johnson.

City manager Roberto Mancini made nine changes to his side, with only Jerome Boateng and Jo retaining their places following the Barclays Premier League victory over West Ham at the weekend. Micah Richards was given the captain's armband.

Jo was partnered up front by Alex Nimely, the 19-year-old handed his first start by Mancini.

Job done, Mancini's men ended a tough few days on a good note with a decent European performance and the draw they needed to top the group. (*Sun*)

Roberto Mancini was held to a stalemate on his return to Italy. (***Daily Mail***)

City finally get mo-Jo working to be top dogs

Roberto Mancini was held to stalemate on his return to Italy as Jo salvaged a vital draw for Manchester City in the Stadio Olimpico.

Teenage star Niccolo Gianetti put Juventus ahead with a 43rd minute strike but Jo made amends for a string of misses with a neat leveller after 76 minutes. Mancini left some of his biggest stars at home but still named a strong side handing a first start to young Alex Nimely but in truth it seemed both sides had lost their way on a freezing night in Turin but it was Juventus who landed the first blow when they struck shortly before the break however Jo made up for his wastefulness with 16 minutes to go when he took Johnson's cross and turned neatly before burying a low drive into the bottom corner.

MANAGEMENT VIEW

It was very important to finish top of the group. We have a chance to go all the way, but it is important to have a good draw for the next round, and after that we will see.

I did not expect to play against such a strong Juventus team. Our players showed good character, and we hope to carry on like this. But in the end I think we deserved a draw, minimum. (**Roberto Mancini**)

I have known him for five years.

He played against Inter in the Champions League and scored two goals. He was young, but he was a good player, and he is still a good player.

He played the last two games for us and did not score. But he has done very well, so I am pleased he has scored. (**Roberto Mancini on Jo**)

ARIS THESSALONIKI 0   MANCHESTER CITY 0

UEFA Europa League
Round of 32 – First Leg, Tuesday 15 February 2011
Kleanthis Vikelidis Stadium
Attendance: 22,000

City Team: Hart, Richards, Boateng, K. Toure, Kolarov, Wright-Phillips (Balotelli), Barry, Y. Toure, Silva, Dzeko (Zabaleta), Tevez
Subs: Given (GK), Kompany, Lescott, Vieira, Jo

Manchester City could not find a way through a resolute Aris Salonika defence as the first leg of the Europa League last-32 tie ended goalless.

Striker Edin Dzeko failed to convert Aleksandar Kolarov's low cross from City's best chance of the first half.

Dzeko's header forced a great save from Michalis Sifakis, before Neto sent a fierce effort just wide for Aris.

Mario Balotelli returned for City as a late substitute and saw a bicycle kick float wide in the dying stages.

The hosts had never lost in 24 European matches at the Kleanthis Vikelidis Stadium

PRESS VIEW

A dreadful game. City were on top for most of the first half, but didn't keep going. Aris were much the better side in the second half; their proud European home record stays intact. (*Guardian*)

Manchester City took a step towards the last 16 of the Europa League by keeping a clean sheet in Greece tonight.

It was a professional performance given that Aris have never be been beaten in 40 years of European competition at the Kleanthis Vikelidis Stadium.

It could have been even better but former Wolfsburg striker Edin Dzeko was out of luck in the second half. (*Sporting Life*)

The walls of the Greek fortress remain unbreached but City should win the battle next week. (*Manchester Evening News*)

Not great but at least it was no Greek Tragedy. Expect City to finish the job back at Eastland's next week. (*Sun*)

UEFA are to investigate after City players complained laser pens were shone into their eyes after the 0-0 draw with Aris. Roberto Mancini confirmed some of his team had been targeted, in particular Edin Dzeko and Aleks Kolarov. (*Manchester Evening News*)

> ### Rob raiders draw blank
> Roberto Mancini's Fab Four failed to produce a hit for misfiring Manchester City. When Mario Balotelli was sent on with 14 minutes left it was the first time he had teamed up with Carlos Tevez, Edin Dzeko and David Silva in a forward line costing just over £100m.
>
> Aris were defending a 25-game unbeaten home record in Europe, stretching back to 1979 but City had more than enough chances to end it, Silva had a shot parried by keeper Michalis Sifakis after seven minutes, Richards had justified appeals for a penalty dismissed when Michel brought him down, Dzeko fluffed a chance when the strikers header from a corner went over the bar.
>
> The second half followed the same pattern as the first with long periods of City possession punctuated by the odd counter attack by the home side, Dzeko was close with two further chances but Aris held out and Mancini and his players were left frustrated.

The players walked out to an unbelievable atmosphere, drums banging, fireworks exploding, and ticker tape streaming down from the masses. The City boys must have felt like they were heading into a battle rather than a football match. (*Manchester Evening News*)

Aris Thessaloniki officials were left red faced after Tuesday's Europa League tie with Manchester City, when it emerged a spoof photo of their opponents had made its way into the match day programme.

MANAGEMENT VIEW
Of course it would have been better for the tie and for ourselves if we had won the game and that is what we tried to do. Their goalkeeper played very well. Now we have another game and if we win we are through to the last 16. (**Roberto Mancini**)

SUPPORTERS' VIEWS
'Poor Game, Poor performance from the officials and both teams.'

'Felt sorry for the diehards, who travelled over to watch that.'

'Not the most exciting game ever. Decent enough result though.'

'City played well with plenty of possession and kept them limited.'

'We did a job, no more, no less, we will at Eastland's next week.'

SUPPORTERS' TALES

Well we all have heard how fervent Greek supporters are and the past troubles with English fans, so it was with some trepidation we that we booked on the official Thomas Cook overnight trip to Salonika.

A mid afternoon arrival meant time to check in at our hotel, which was aptly named 'The City Hotel' – boy does it take ages to check in when 200 fans descend on a little reception all at once.

The rest of the day was spent exploring the bars and cafes off the water front and various squares whilst dealing with the 'lucky lucky' sellers, but they were soon perplexed when asked for Vera Lynns greatest hits or a copy of City winning the Europa League on DVD.

The following morning still gave time for yet another stroll along the water front and the sight of many City fans suffering from the affects of too much alchol and yet another encounter with a 'lucky lucky' man who pointed across the bay to a ship and informed me he would be sailing back to Cyprus later on it so it was my last chance to buy some 'reasonably' priced perfume or if that did not take my liking some 'real' gold bracelets. (Sometimes I feel I must be the luckiest person in the world to come across such bargains.)

There was plenty of confusion regarding the journey to the ground, we had to board the coach to travel literaly 500 yards to the White Tower an ancient monument on the waterfront, where all supporters would have their match tickets checked and their belongings searched, you had to be there to see what a farce that was as not one Greek police man spoke a word of English, as supporters disembarked coaches, leaving their bags behind, were searched and then let back on the coach.

The coaches finally departed after much merriment and arrived at the compact ground, with supporters hearing the news that the official programme had been withdrawn due to an administration error, fortunately I found one that had been dispossessed off, not bad really as they were later selling back home for £180 each.

The whole away end was a joke with bucket seats, a set of stairs that led to a six foot drop unless you had your wits about you, and several drunken City fans did not as they took heavy falls, a single gate to access and egress the seats and a food bar which was a table selling sandwiches and Coke.

The game was a non event and our misery was compounded because after the game we were kept behind for almost an hour and it gave a few Aris fans their moments of fame as they proceeded to throw bottles of water at us whilst the local police just stood around. **(Jessica Waldon)**

MANCHESTER CITY 3   ARIS THESSALONIKI 0

Goal Scorers: Dzeko (2), Y. Toure
UEFA Europa League
Round of 32 – Second Leg, Thursday 24 February 2011
City of Manchester Stadium
Attendance: 36,748

> **City Team:**
> Hart, Boateng, Kompany (Zabaleta), Lescott, Kolarov, Silva (Wright-Phillips), Y. Toure, Barry, Tevez (Vieira), Dzeko, Balotelli
> Subs: Taylor (GK), Jo, K. Toure, Wabara

PRESS VIEW

Edin Dzeko scored two early goals and Yaya Toure added a third to ease Manchester City past Aris Salonika and into the Europa League last 16.

City were held to a 0-0 draw in the first leg but £27m January signing Dzeko slotted the hosts in front before curling in a second soon after.

After Mario Balotelli's shot hit a post, Toure fired home via a deflection to seal a 3-0 aggregate win. (**BBC**)

Aris' best performers were their astonishing fans, just as they were in creating a white hot atmosphere for the first leg. They were a riot of noise and colour who waved flags, banners and even the odd inflatable banana. The visitors may have been beaten early but the travelling support never flagged. (*Manchester Evening News*)

The Greeks contributed to their own downfall initially, a poor reward for the impressive loving support that 6,000 raucous travelling fans poured down on their team of honest but limited toilers. (**MCFC**)

For the first time, Roberto Mancini started a match with Carlos Tevez, Edin Dzeko, David Silva and Mario Balotelli – respectively purchased for £32 million, £27 million, £24 million and £22.5 million – alongside each other. Against meagre opposition, the result was a formality. Two Dzeko goals in the first 12 minutes killed the game; Yaya Toure added gloss late on. (*Daily Telegraph*)

Roberto Mancini's side could and should have pressed home their advantage more but the gulf in class between the two sides was clear and sufficient to seal the result.
The disappointing goalless trip to Greece planted seeds of doubt regarding the credentials of City but with this display in front of their own fans, all those doubts were banished with an assured and comfortable performance. (*GOAL*)

Mancini, already with six players side-lined with injury, suffered another blow when Vincent Kompany, City's most accomplished defender this season, went off with a hip injury. (*Daily Mirror*)

> ### City's Ed boy Dzeko gets early cut
> Two early goals from Edin Dzeko set Manchester City on their way to the last 16 of the Europa league. The Bosnia-Herzegovina striker netted twice in the first 12 minutes to kill off spirited Greek outfit Aris Salonika, his first goals in Europe since his £27 million January move from Wolfsburg.
>
> Following a goalless draw in the first leg, Dzeko took just seven minutes to open the scoring, profiting from Nikolaos Lazaridis' error to fire home. He then bagged a brilliant second five minutes later before Yaya Toure added a fierce late third.

A devastating opening burst from Dzeko ensured City were Edin into the next round. It was a joyous occasion for Roberto Mancini's men but a tragedy for the Greeks. (*Sun*)

It was the perfect result for Mancini, who knows his side have a good chance of going on to win this competition. (*Daily Star*)

MANAGEMENT & PLAYER VIEW

First half we played very well. It was important to start well. It was the first time those three strikers had played together, and they need to do it again. Kiev is a big team who have always played in the Champions League. They will be difficult. (**Roberto Mancini**)

I'm very happy. It was not as easy as the result shows. The early goals were very important. I can play much better though. I should have scored a hat-trick. (**Edin Dzeko**)

DYNAMO KIEV 2   MANCHESTER CITY 0

UEFA Europa League
Round of 16 – First Leg, Thursday 10 March 2011
Valeriy Lobanovskiy Stadium
Attendance: 16,000

> **City Team:** Hart, Richards, Kompany, Lescott, Zabaleta,, Y. Toure, Barry, Kolarov (Wright-Phillips), Dzeko, Balotelli, (Tevez), Silva
> Subs: Taylor (GK), Boateng, Boyata, Vieira, De Jong

Goals from Andriy Shevchenko and Oleh Gusev gave Dynamo Kiev a significant lead to take to Manchester after the Europa League last-16 first leg.

Former Chelsea and AC Milan striker Shevchenko was lively throughout and opened the scoring when he bundled in Andriy Yarmolenko's twenty-fifth-minute cross.

David Silva had City's best chance but could not direct Pablo Zabaleta's scuffed cross towards goal.

Gusev rifled Artem Milevskiy's flick-on into the corner to cap a fine display.

PRESS VIEW

The temperature was several degrees below zero, City's midfield operated as if semi-frozen and a suddenly allergy stricken Mario Balotelli departed early, feeling sickly.

All in all a Ukrainian night illuminated by Andrey Shevchenko's clever feet and perfect balance proved pretty awful for Roberto Mancini's side who have much to do if they are to survive the second leg at Eastland's

City seemed to freeze in the sub-zero temperatures and now face a huge task in the return leg. (*Sun*)

MANAGEMENT VIEW

If we want to get to the quarter finals, we have to play better than we did and defend better. I think we played well, but made two mistakes, two big mistakes and paid the price. (**Roberto Mancini**)

SUPPORTERS' TALES – An Allergy to Grass

The last 16 of the Europa League season 2010/11 saw City drawn against Ukrainian giants, Dynamo Kiev. As Kiev was so far away Thomas Cook put on an overnight stay trip in Kiev itself. The usual early trip out of Manchester saw us land in Kiev at around 10 a.m. It was cold, bitterly cold.

The coaches took us to our hotel and we checked in. The lifts to the rooms were directly opposite a door for the joined strip club, Star Bar. We took it upon ourselves to leave the hotel straight away and explore the city. Map in hand we strode the streets trying to find local landmarks, this was made extremely difficult for us as our map was In the English alphabet and the street signs had the Ukrainian alphabet. We decided to walk up to the stadium and have a look around; it was in the midst of a park dug down into the ground. All fenced off too, not the most welcoming of places.

We walked around the park for a while, visiting the club shop in the process, before heading to the edge of the park where we came across a viewpoint high in the park overlooking a huge forest, breathtaking.

We made our way back into the City centre bumping into numerous packs of stray dogs in the process. Kiev was such a different experience than anything I had ever done before, clearly still run by an iron fist and under the steel curtain too. The police were on every street corner, guarding toilet blocks, and monuments. Everything. The city itself was stunning, a modern, vibrant City with fantastic new architecture mixed in with old historic buildings. The best was yet to come though as underneath the roads and shops on the surface was a massive underground mall built due to the severe weather conditions that Kiev suffers from. The mall was huge and had absolutely everything in it you could need. It was fascinating to see how the natives to Ukraine went about their lives. A totally different and amazing culture to anything I had ever witnessed before. A country that had only become a republic in the year I was born (formally a Communist country under the Soviet Union until 1991) the vast difference to England was clear. European Football has always been a great excuse to get away and as the saying goes 'travel broadens the mind'. This statement is true, I have visited many countries and cities in my brief 20 year history and the Ukraine is the most fascinating I have ever been too. I was hooked.

We made our way back to the hotel after eating in a local fast food chain McFoxy's. We walked past the Star Bar that was joined to the hotel greeted by a life size cut out of Cristiano Ronaldo in a United shirt; this was not going to go down well with the small band of travelling City fans.

The next day came fast and we woke to the sound of car horns as there was gridlock on the manic streets below (there was a car parking block right in the middle of the road!). We hung around for a while until the coaches came to pick us up, we put our bags on the coach and waited to depart to the ground. We were taken to the ground early on the Thursday and were left to our own devices with the strict instructions to be back at the coach point an hour before kick-off.

The time came to go to the drop off point and wait to be escorted to the ground. When we got there the scenes were just crazy, a group of policemen were awaiting our arrival and the ushered into a square like formation. Flanking us from all sides, they then preceded to march us down the slippery iced over hill, down the iciest of steps and into the ground behind the Kiev fans. We were not allowed to break rank, nor speak to the police. Were we really going to watch a football match or were we being escorted to prison cells? We took our seats after being guided to the away fans section and wrapped up in our coats as the temperatures dipped well below zero.

The ground was an open bowl type of stadium which didn't help the conditions. It is worth noting that this game was played at the smaller of the two stadiums that Dynamo Kiev play in. The Lobanovskiy Dynamo stadium is the smaller and holds 16,873 people, while the Olimpiysky National Sports Complex holds an impressive 70,050.

The game was that of a disappointment for City and their travelling fans. We barely troubled Dynamo Kiev and never really looked like scoring, however this was not the same for Dynamo who had beaten Besiktas 8-1 on aggregate in the previous round. They took the lead on 25 minutes when Andriy Shevchenko scored his 67th goal in European football tapping in a cross unmarked past Joe Hart.

Mario Balotelli had a game he would not want to remember as he was forced off in the second half (after failing to make it out on time for the restart anyway) with an injury which he seemed to indicate was due to an allergy to the grass on the pitch in Kiev!

Kiev pressed on in the second leg with City failing to cope with the front four of the Ukrainian giants and although we had a good spell after the introduction of Carlos Tevez we failed to score and it cost us as Kiev's Gusev latched onto a cross to volley spectacularly past Hart.

The game ended 2-0 to the Ukrainians and there was a lot to be unhappy about from the City performance, having failed to score an away goal the task in Manchester was going to be an uphill one when the teams would play in the return fixture.

We filtered back to the coaches marched by the police and were then escorted back to the airport ready for the long and unhappy journey back to Manchester. **(Daniel Waldon)**

MANCHESTER CITY 1   DYNAMO KIEV 0

Goal Scorer: Kolarov
UEFA Europa League
Round of 16 – Second Leg, Thursday 17 March 2011
City of Manchester Stadium
Attendance: 27,816

City Team: Hart, Richards, Kompany, Kolarov (Milner), Barry (A. Johnson), Lescott, Silva (Dzeko), Tevez, De Jong, Y. Toure, Balotelli
Subs: Taylor (GK), Wright-Phillips, Vieira, Boyata

Ten-man Manchester City were dumped out of the Europa League despite earning a 1-0 second-leg win over Dynamo Kiev.

City dominated the first half but Mario Balotelli scooped over from three yards and missed with a header from 12 yards.

Striker Balotelli was sent off for a foul on Goran Popov before the break, giving City a tough task to overcome their two-goal first-leg deficit.

Aleksandar Kolarov fired in low from 20 yards to give them hope but City failed to trouble Kiev in the second half.

PRESS VIEW
While the brave 10 men of Manchester City fought to the very last to extend their European future, Mario Balotelli's X Rated challenge left City with too much to do and saw them crash out of the Europa League. *(Sun)*

The Ukraine side looked nervy, in contrast to the confident display seen in the first leg, and were content to hit City on the break – although they did this with very little success. *(BBC)*

Mario shame as City crash

Manchester City's European dream turned into a nightmare, thanks to Mario Balotelli's brainstorm at Eastland's. Balotelli was shown a straight red card for his outrageous kung-fu kick at Goran Popov, but it was Roberto Mancini's men who were booted out of the Europa League as Dynamo Kiev had the last laugh to book their place in the last eight.

Balotelli's sending off after just 37 minutes, left City with too much to do despite Aleksandar Kolarov's fine strike which gave them some hope.

Richards could have hauled City level but headed Silva's free kick over on 50 minutes and Shovkovskiy saved well at the feet of Silva as City became desperate. Lescott had to head clear off his own line on 67 minutes to keep his side in with a sniff. Mancini then threw on Adam Johnson but there was little the England star could do to stamp his mark on a game ruined by petulant fouls and the referee's whistle, which also resulted in eight bookings.

MANAGEMENT & PLAYER VIEW

I'm disappointed because this was a difficult game and you can't have a stupid red card like this.

It's a problem for Mario because he can be a fantastic player, but when he does stupid things like tonight, it's difficult for me, for him and for the team. **(Roberto Mancini, who is expected to fine Balotelli two weeks' wages totalling £240,000)**

As soon as we went down to 10 men, it was a very difficult game. If we haven't qualified, it is down to one detail. **(Vincent Kompany)**

2011-12 CHAMPIONS LEAGUE/EUROPA LEAGUE

MANCHESTER CITY 1   NAPOLI 1

Goal Scorer: Kolarov

UEFA Champions League
Group A – Match Day 1, Wednesday 14 September 2011
City of Manchester Stadium (Etihad)
Attendance: 44,026

City Team: Hart, Zabaleta, Kompany, Lescott, Kolarov (Clichy), Y. Toure, Barry, Nasri (A. Johnson), Aguero, Silva, Dzeko (Tevez)
Subs: Pantillimon (GK), Richards, Savic, K. Toure

PRESS VIEW

Manchester City had to come from behind on their UEFA Champions League debut to earn a 1-1 draw with Napoli at the Etihad Stadium.

Both sides struck the woodwork in a goalless first-half but a neat break from the Italian visitors saw Edinson Cavani grab the opening goal on 69 minutes.

The lead lasted just six minutes, however, as City responded through Aleksandar Kolarov's sublime free-kick, which left Napoli keeper Morgan De Sanctis rooted to the spot. **(SKY)**

Roberto Mancini's men might have swept all before them in the Premier League this season but they found things a lot harder against the Italian side on their return to elite European football after a 43-year absence. **(BBC)**

It was a bit nervy for City on their Champions League debut which almost cost them. But defeat would have been cruel. **(*Sun*)**

MANAGEMENT VIEW

I sensed before the game that we were nervous. We all wanted to win so much. Maybe there was too much desire. Now that the game is out of our system, maybe we can go to Munich and relax. (**Roberto Mancini**)

Certainly after the Cavani goal we could have closed the game. There we did something wrong but I say this only because we are perfectionists. After starting a little tense we began to express our own game. In the first half we divided the chances but in the second half we were superior. (**Walter Mazzarri, Napoli coach**)

BAYERN MUNICH 2   MANCHESTER CITY 0

UEFA Champions League
Group A – Match Day 2, Tuesday 27 September 2011
Allianz Arena, Munich
Attendance: 66,000

City Team:
Hart, Richards, Kompany, K. Toure, Clichy, Y. Toure, Barry (Kolarov), Nasri (Milner), Aguero, Silva, Dzeko (De Jong)
Subs:
Pantilimon (GK), Zabaleta, Lescott, Tevez

Carlos Tevez effectively went on strike after being asked to come on early in the second half in what was an unprecedented act of defiance.

Roberto Mancini later declared 'Tevez would never play for the club again'.

Manchester City can confirm that striker Carlos Tevez has been suspended until further notice for a maximum period of two weeks. The player's suspension is pending a full review into his alleged conduct during City's 2-0 defeat to Bayern Munich.

Manchester City's big night in the Champions League ended with failure on the pitch and problems off it for manager Roberto Mancini as Bayern Munich maintained their remarkable record over English teams.

Although City looked capable of becoming only the second team to beat the German giants on their own ground in European combat for half an hour, two Mario Gomez goals in eight minutes before the break turned the tie on its head. The whole match was however over shadowed by the Carlos Tevez saga.

City kick out Tevez

Furious boss Roberto Mancini has told Carlos Tevez he will NEVER play for the club again after the argentine sub refused to go on in Munich.

The Manchester City boss was seething after he called Tevez off the bench in the second half as City trailed 2-0, but the striker would not go on.

Mancini will speak to chairman Khaldoon al Mubarak to support his action and it is now certain Tevez, who asked for a move in the summer, will be booted out when the January transfer window opens. Mancini said "With me he is finished, he refused to go on the pitch, but I decide this not Carlos. If one player earns a lot of money playing for Manchester City in the Champions League and he behaves like this, for me he can't play-never. I'm really disappointed that a top player refuses to go and help his team mates".

Many supporters flooded various media sources with their thoughts, here are a selection:

'I hope I never see Tevez play in a City shirt again. He should be fined the maximum and left out of the squad.'
'Get rid of Tevez. What an absolute disgrace.'
'Get Tevez out as soon as possible, he must never play for City again.'

PRESS VIEW

This was supposed to be the final frontier for City.
    Instead, they discovered just how steep the learning curve is to make the transition from Champions League qualifiers to actual contenders. (*Sporting Life*)
A European lesson for City and they will have it all to do to get through the group now. (*Sun*)

Until the goals City appeared to be comfortable, but Gomes changed that. (*Daily Star*)

MANAGEMENT VIEW

Maybe at the moment this team (Bayern) is too strong for us but we have a chance to go through. We still have four games to go and all is not lost. (**Roberto Mancini**)

We scored the goals at the right time and we were very comfortable after that. We were nervous to start with and did not really believe in ourselves. Ribery was world class today. Everything went are way in the second half. (**Jupp Heynckes, Bayern coach**)

SUPPORTERS' VIEWS

'Sorry Mancini, you only have yourself to blame. With that set up you were always going to lose the midfield.'

'We are in with the big boys now and this will happen along the learning curve. But we don't become a bad side overnight.'

'Beaten by a far better team, we should have had two penalties, but after the first 20 minutes we were never in it.'

'Bit of a football lesson but just have to dust it off and get going again.'

'Very disappointed.'

MANCHESTER CITY 2   VILLARREAL 1

Goal scorers: Aguero, Marchena (OG)
UEFA Champions League
Group A – Match Day 3, Tuesday 18 October 2011
City of Manchester Stadium
Attendance: 42,236

City Team: Hart, Zabaleta, Kompany, Lescott, Kolarov, De Jong (Aguero), Y. Toure, A. Johnson (Barry), Silva, Nasri (Milner), Dzeko
Subs: Pantilimon (GK), Richards, Savic, Clichy

PRESS VIEW

Sergio Aguero's winner in the dying seconds rescued Manchester City as they came from behind to claim their first Champions League win.

Roberto Mancini's side looked set for more frustration after Villarreal belied their poor La Liga form to leave City on the brink of a third game without victory in the group stage.

Cani had set the tone for an uncomfortable evening when he gave Villarreal the lead after only four minutes and City's only response was an own goal from Carlos Marchena just before the interval.

But deep into stoppage time, and with what turned out to be almost the final kick of the game, substitute Aguero arrived at the far post to turn Pablo Zabaleta's cross past Diego Lopez to revive City's hopes of reaching the knockout phase. (**BBC**)

Money can buy you most things. Not love, mind. Nor Champions League comfort. That was a huge struggle for City, but they have their first ever win in this competition and are now right back in the group. (*Daily Telegraph*)

Sergio Aguero came off the bench to fire Manchester City to a dramatic victory and that breathed fresh life into City's hopes of making the Champions League knockout stages. (*Daily Star*)

It was a struggle for City against a team they would have expected to roll over. But, thankfully for them, Aguero came up trumps. (*Sun*)

MANAGEMENT VIEW

I think we deserved to win because we had a lot of chances to score but Villarreal were very dangerous on the counter attack. When you play in the Champions League for the first time you need to improve game after game. We needed to win and I think tonight, after this game, we can do better. (**Roberto Mancini**)

We competed very well and I think we should congratulate the players for the great job they have done, whatever the outcome, with which we are obviously not happy when it occurs in the last minute. (**Juan Carlos Garrido, Villarreal Coach**)

VILLARREAL 0   MANCHESTER CITY 3

Goal Scorers: Yaya Toure (2), Balotelli (P)
UEFA Champions League
Group A – Match Day 4, Wednesday 2 November 2011
El Madrigal
Attendance: 24,235

City Team: Hart, Zabaleta, Kompany, Savic, Clichy, Y. Toure (Aguero), De Jong, Nasri, Silva (A. Johnson), Milner, Balotelli (Kolarov)
Subs: Pantillimon (GK), Lescott, Barry, Dzeko

Did You Know?
Man City have scored in all seven of their European games against Spanish sides and have now scored two or more goals in five of them.

Manchester City moved into second spot in Group A of the Champions League with a comfortable victory at Villarreal.

Roberto Mancini's side will now qualify for the knockout stages if they win in Napoli in their next game.

Yaya Toure gave City the lead when he slotted in from just inside the area, before Mario Balotelli doubled the advantage from the spot after he was fouled by Mateo Musacchio in the box.

Yaya made it 3-0 when he jinked past Carlos Marchena before firing in.

It was as easy an exercise as the score line suggests

PRESS VIEW
The Spanish side are struggling in La Liga but looked unruffled during that opening period. They worked hard as a team to suffocate City's danger men of David Silva, Samir Nasri and Balotelli, who tried their utmost to conjure something out of nothing. **(BBC)**

The only discomfort Roberto Mancini felt came in the form of the bang on the head that required him to watch a significant part of this game with an icepack held against his crown. "The dugout here is very dangerous," the Manchester City manager winced afterwards, but otherwise this was a pain-free evening for his team, beating the Spaniards for the second time in two weeks to invigorate hope of qualifying for the knockout phase

Villarreal were obliging opponents and will almost certainly finish with the group's wooden spoon, having not taken a single point so far, but there was still something impressively professional and disciplined about the way City ran out easy winners. **(*Guardian*)**

At last a European performance of stature from Mnachester City. At last something to build on.

Manager Roberto Mancini may have ended the game with an ice pack on his head after banging it on the dugout roof but that, frankly, was as uncomfortable as it got for the Italian and his players against a woeful Villarreal team at Estadio El Madrigal on Wednesday night. (*Daily Mail*)

Manchester City make light work of an under strength Villarreal as two goals from Yaya Toure and another from in-form Mario Balotelli gives Roberto Mancini's side as comfortable an away win in the Champions League as they are ever likely to enjoy. (*Daily Telegraph*)

Yaya Toure sank the Yellow Submarines and steered Manchester City's European campaign back on course. (*Sun*)

MANAGEMENT VIEW

Villarreal were missing four or five important players but it is always difficult to win away in the Champions League. We had 65 per cent of ball possession, we scored three goals. I think this was important for our confidence. I think we have improved. (**Roberto Mancini**)

All the players have shown a great attitude. With that and players recovering from injuries, we can get better results. (**Juan Carlos Garrido, Villarreal Coach**)

SUPPORTERS' VIEWS

'Another record broken by City, the first English team to win in Villarreal and we equalled our previous best away win in Europe.'

'Good professional performance and a clean sheet at last.'

'Very important win for City. It's in our own hands, great performance by the whole team.

'Job done. Not much more to say.'

'It turned out to be an easy victory for the lads. As per usual the fans were immense in their support of the Blues.'

NAPOLI 2   MANCHESTER CITY 1

Goal Scorer: Balotelli
UEFA Champions League
Group A – Match Day 5, Tuesday 22 November 2011
Stadio San Paolo
Attendance: 57,575

City Team: Hart, Zabaleta (A. Johnson), Kompany, Lescott, Kolarov, De Jong (Nasri), Y. Toure, Milner, Silva, Dzeko (Aguero, Balotelli
Subs: Pantillimon (GK), Clichy, Richards, Barry

It is back to the drawing board for the Blues after they came up short in their biggest Champions League test to date.

The attacking threat which has torn apart the best Premier League defences this season was only sporadically seen in Stadio San Paolo

Edinson Cavani's near-post header put the Italians into the lead before Mario Balotelli levelled when he tapped home from two yards out.

But Cavani's low shot early in the second half saw off City.

PRESS VIEW

Manchester City's Champions League hopes are hanging by a thread; they are now third in Group A going into the last game and must hope that they can beat Bayern Munich and Napoli slip up at Villarreal. (*Manchester Evening News*)

This was an incredible game. Everyone who was at San Paulo will tell their children and grandchildren of the time they saw an excellent team that played without fear and were able to beat Manchester City. (*La Gazzetta dello Sport*)

Mario Strike not enough as Mancini's men taught tough lesson

Manchester City's hopes of reaching the last 16 of the Champions League suffered a potentially fatal blow as Edinson Cavani's double set up a must win showdown for Roberto Mancini's side in their final group game against Bayern Munich.

Victory would have sent the Premier League leaders through but Cavani's strikes and two late missed chances from City goal scorer Mario Balotelli means Mancini's men must beat Bayern and hope Napoli fail to beat group whipping boys Villarreal. City were frequently stretched by the fast breaking Italians and were lucky to escape early on when Marek Hamsik nodded straight at Joe Hart. Cavani's glancing header from a corner squeezed past a flapping Hart at his near post in the 17th minute but minutes later City were level. Salvatore Aronica's poor clearance found David Silva whose shot was parried by Morgan de Sanctis before Balotelli tapped into an empty net.

Aleksander Kolarov went close before the break but in the 49th minute Cavani side footed a low first time shot past the slow-to-ground Hart.

Hart kept out Ezequiel Lavezzi and Christian Maggio in a frantic finish while Hamsik struck a post. Balotelli, though, could have earned at least a point for City, firing straight at De Sanctis when through on goal and then nodding over from close range.

MANAGEMENT VIEW

We should still believe because it is my opinion that Villarreal can get a result against Napoli. I don't think they will end up with no points and I certainly believe they are capable of a draw so we still have a chance, even though we are relying on another team. (**Roberto Mancini**)

Winning when you have only one result in mind, as we did tonight, is incredible, in games like tonight's, you can find the energy that you cannot even think you have. (**Walter Mazzarri, Napoli coach**)

MANCHESTER CITY 2   BAYERN MUNICH 0

Goal Scorers: Silva, Yaya Toure
UEFA Champions League
Group A – Match Day 6, Wednesday 7 December 2011
City of Manchester Stadium
Attendance: 46,002

City Team: Hart, Savic, Kompany, Lescott, Clichy, Barry, Y. Toure (Balotelli), Silva (A. Johnson), Aguero, Nasri, Dzeko (De Jong)
Subs: Pantillimon (GK), Zabaleta, Milner, K. Toure

PRESS VIEW

Manchester City's Champions League campaign ended in disappointment as they beat Bayern Munich but finished behind Napoli, who secured the win they needed against Villarreal.

The odds were always against City after their defeat in Napoli- but they were offered brief hope of reaching the knockout phase as goals either side of the interval from David Silva and Yaya Toure put them in command against Bayern.

For a few tantalising moments City looked set to claim the precious qualifying place as Napoli struggled to break down Villarreal, but Etihad Stadium was plunged into eerie silence as news of the Italians' goals in Spain filtered through. (**BBC**)

Mancini can absorb the lessons and regard the Europa League, no matter how it is viewed elsewhere, as an opportunity to win another trophy. It will not be a priority but City have the strength of squad to make a go of it. **(MCFC BLOG)**

For a long part of the night Manchester City dared to believe that everything was falling in place. They were beating the mighty Bayern Munich, looking good to add more goals and building towards a moment of rare euphoria. But then the news began to seep through from Villarreal and all the excitement was replaced by a sudden, damp silence.

The cold, harsh truth is that Napoli's second-half goals at El Madrigal mean that City will not be in the Champions League when the men in suits at Uefa convene for the draw on Friday week.

They will go into the last 32 full of regret, however much they try to put on a brave face, and it will probably only heighten their frustration that they are being downgraded on the back of beating one of the genuine European powerhouses. City have accumulated 10 points in Group A, which is usually the amount needed to qualify. (*Guardian*)

As the City fans sang at the end. We'll be here on Thursday nights, and they will, but we will be back in the Champions League again soon, and this team will have learned from their mistakes. **(MCFC WEB)**

Next time we will be wiser and stronger

City duly completed their part of the qualification equation by beating an under strength Bayern Munich but it was not enough to qualify for the next stages.

Goals from David Silva and Yaya Toure underlined manager Mancini's view that his team are improving as a European force, and this victory put down something of a marker that they will be back a wiser, stronger and tighter unit next season, but for now City reluctantly join a list of teams who have achieved the accepted 10-point benchmark of qualification from the group stages yet still failed to qualify

City thought they had taken the lead in the 15th minute when Silva's free kick sailed over everyone's heads and into the far corner of the net, only for the referee to decide that Joleon Lescott had impeded the goal keeper Jorg Butt, but City's methodical patient approach paid off however after 37 minutes when Silva turned goal taker, Dzeko flicked a pass from Gareth Barry into the path of the impish Silva, he took a touch to go past a defender before swivelling on the edge of the area to send a crisp half volley past Butt and into the corner of the net and City had to wait only seven minutes into the second half for their next goal, a precise passing move involving Yaya Toure, Sergio Aguero and Dzeko opened up the Bayern defence and saw Toure run onto Dzeko's pass and coolly stab the ball past Butt.

Never a problem for City against a half-strength Bayern. But they only have themselves to blame for going out. (**Sun**)

A disastrous night in Manchester for the Champions League but the Big Blue moon is still smiling. City's performance was that of a club close to stamping their authority home and abroad in this competition. (***Daily Star***)

Silva lining not enough for City and Roberto Mancini's men will have to wait another year before they can try to take their place right up there with Europe's elite. (***Daily Star***)

MANAGEMENT VIEW

With 10 points, 99 per cent of the time, you will qualify for the next phase; I think we now need to concentrate on trying to win the Europa League. It will be good for the club if we can get to the final and win it. (**Roberto Mancini**)

I am pleased with my team's performance. It was not going to be easy with such a new line up and City were highly motivated. But we were in a difficult group and we won it. (**Jupp Heynckes, Bayern coach**)

SUPPORTERS' VIEWS

'Good try; good goals our time will come.'

'We did what we had to do but had no control over our destiny. It is a great experience for our team and club.'

'Well done boys for beating Bayern, at the end it was out of our hands, but this team will grow stronger next year.'

'Nothing to be ashamed of. Disappointing I know but you made the club proud.'

'I don't know about you but I'm proud of our boys.'

FC PORTO 1   MANCHESTER CITY 2

Goal Scorers: Aguero, Pereira (OG)
Europa League
Round of 32 – First Leg, Thursday 16 February 2012
Estadio do Dragao
Attendance: 47,417

City Team: Hart, Richards, Kompany, Lescott, Clichy, De Jong, Barry, Nasri (Zabaleta), Y. Toure, Silva (Kolarov), Balotelli (Aguero)
Subs: Pantillimon (GK), Savic, Pizarro, Dzeko

Substitute Sergio Aguero hit a dramatic late Europa League winner as Manchester City came from behind to beat holders Porto in the first leg of the last 32.

City trailed to Silvestre Varela's close-range effort following a powerful run and cross by Hulk.

But the visitors impressed and deservedly equalised when Alvaro Pereira deflected Yaya Toure's cross into his own net off his shoulder.

They sealed victory when Aguero tapped home following Toure's cross.

PRESS VIEW

On a memorable night for Roberto Mancini's side at the Estadio do Dragao, the Premier League leaders did not look like a team of players who felt sorry for themselves as they returned to the continental stage for the first time since being denied a place in the knockout stages of the Champions League by Napoli and Bayern Munich. (**BBC**)

It was the Blues finest European night for some time as they turned over a team that rarely loses in their impressive stadium. Porto have proven European pedigree and are notoriously difficult to beat in their home town. (*Manchester Evening News*)

Wednesday's second leg should be a formality thanks to City's best away win in Europe in decades. They can take great confidence from their display, which was the perfect response to their Champions League exit. (*Daily Mirror*)

City's best European away day for a long time has them on the brink of sending the holders crashing. (*Sun*)

Late Serg as City pass the port by coming from behind to record an impressive win over the holders. (*Daily Star*)

MANAGEMENT VIEW

I think that we played a good game, we played very well. In the first half we had three or four goal scoring chances. We were really unlucky.

Aguero is the City Champion

Roberto Mancini's belief that Manchester City were unlucky to go out of the Champions League was given further credence in the Estadio do Dragao, City showed they had learned their lessons from earlier defeats by coming from behind to record an impressive win over holders Porto.

They kept their composure after Silvestre Valera had given Porto a half time lead, then hit back in an improved second half display through Alvaro Pereira's own goal before a late winner from substitute Sergio Aguero.

City fell behind after 27 minutes when Micah Richards allowed Hulk to deliver a low cross from the left and Vincent Kompany was slow to react to the danger, with Varela stealing half a yard to convert the cross at the near post. City sharpened up their act, with Richards setting the tone when his shot struck the post and Samir Nasri and Balotelli both had shots saved by Porto keeper Helton and City got stronger as the game wore on Pereira inadvertently put City level, Toure's deep cross from the left, so Balotelli un-nerve Pereira to the extent that he knocked the ball past the keeper and with Aguero on for Balotelli he grabbed a late winner.

In the second half we played very well. We played as we know. We had seven, eight chances to score and we didn't give any chances to Porto, which is important because Porto is a top team.

I think we won the game very well. We had more chances to score than them. **(Roberto Mancini)**

We scored a good goal but in the second half Manchester City started better, they created a lot of difficulties for us. They played well on the counter attack. **(Vitor Pereira, Porto Coach)**

SUPPORTERS' VIEWS

'Fantastic performance in a very open game.'

'Given Porto's formidable home record that was a really good result.'

'In parts excellent but very poor in others. Too many silly bookings which leaves us with seven player's one yellow card away from suspension.'

MANCHESTER CITY 4   FC PORTO 0

Goal Scorers: Aguero, Dzeko, Silva, Pizarro
UEFA Europa League
Round of 32 – Second Leg, Wednesday 22 February 2012
City of Manchester Stadium
Attendance: 39,548

City Team: Hart, Richards, Kompany, Lescott, Clichy, Barry (Milner), De Jong, Nasri (Dzeko), Y. Toure, Silva, Aguero (Pizarro)
Subs: Pantilimon (GK), Zabaleta, Savic, Balotelli

PRESS VIEW

Sergio Aguero was again the headline act as Manchester City sealed an impressive win over holders Porto to reach the last 16 of the Europa League.

The Argentine scored City's first-leg winner and here he gave them the lead after just 19 seconds with a low shot.

He then turned creator for Edin Dzeko to score a goal which Porto's Rolando was sent off for protesting against.

With the tie won, City romped home thanks to well-worked goals from David Silva and substitute David Pizarro. **(BBC)**

A quite remarkable finish to a tie much tighter than the scoreline suggests sent City surging through to the last 16 of the Europa League as the bemused holders reeled out at the Etihad Stadium.

Porto fell behind in just 18 seconds to a strike from man of the match Sergio Aguero, but they more than held their own thereafter until the Blues produced a grandstand finish and three more goals in the last 15 minutes. **(MCFC)**

Although the decisive goals came late, the result did not flatter the Barclays Premier League leaders.

The Portuguese champions may have controlled the game at times but they lacked a cutting edge and Roberto Mancini's side always looked more threatening in attack. **(*Sporting Life*)**

It was a typically rainy night in Manchester, but things were far from gloomy for Roberto Mancini. After Porto defender Rolando received a second yellow card, City made it a rout. **(*Metro*)**

NOTE: City lodged a complaint after Balotelli was subjected to monkey taunts during the first leg of their Europa League last-32 tie at the Estadio do Dragao on February 16. There were outbreaks of monkey chanting throughout the game, which City won 2-1, but it appeared most noticeable when Balotelli was substituted 12 minutes from time. Porto coach Vitor Pereira later claimed there may have been a misunderstanding and that fans were actually chanting 'Hulk, Hulk, Hulk' at the club's star player.

A Uefa statement said: 'The Uefa Control and Disciplinary Body has imposed a fine of 20,000 Euros on FC Porto for racist conduct of their supporters (Article 11bis – Discrimination and similar conduct) at their first-leg round of 32 Uefa Europa League match against Manchester City FC on 16 February in Porto.

'The club has the right to appeal within three days from the dispatch of the decision.'

Forget Carlos Tevez, Argentine players are back in the good books of Manchester City fans, thanks to Sergio Aguero. (*Sun*)

MANAGEMENT VIEW

It was a good night but it was not easy. We had other chances to score but we didn't score, and when you don't score, you can have other problems.

It is not easy to beat Porto, they are one of the top teams in Europe and I am happy that we are going to the next stage.

We want to try to go to the final if possible but it will be difficult because the Europa League has top squads - Manchester United, Valencia, Schalke – it is like the Champions League.

For this reason it will be difficult but we want to try. (**Roberto Mancini**)

Up until the second Manchester City goal, Porto were the best team. We played much better but we know Manchester City have a good team and they used the counter-attack well.

They have great players up front and the second goal caused us difficulties. We wanted to change the game but the sending off changed it in favour of Manchester City.

Someone who has not seen the match is wrong in their opinion if they think City have dominated the game. The scoreline does not show what happened on the pitch. (**Vitor Pereira, Porto coach**)

SUPPORTERS' VIEWS

'A terrific performance from everybody tonight. Loved the celebrations. A team that wanted to die for each other. We can go on and win this competition.'

'That was a good performance against a quality side. Other than the first half hour we were untroubled and looked solid.'

'Brilliant performance for all the boys even though we were under pressure for part of the game.'

SPORTING LISBON 1   MANCHESTER CITY 0

UEFA Europa League
Round of 16 – First Leg, Thursday 8 March 2012
Jose Alvalade Stadium, Lisbon
Attendance: 34,371

City Team: Hart, Clichy, Kompany (Lescott), Toure, Kolarov, Milner, De Jong, Barry (Nasri), Silva, Aguero, Dzeko (Balotelli)
Subs Not Used: Pantilimon, Pizarro, Johnson, Savic

PRESS VIEW

Manchester City must overturn a one-goal deficit to reach the Europa League quarter-finals after suffering a last-16 first-leg defeat to Sporting Lisbon.

It was a frustrating night for City, who were out of sorts against a well-organised and incisive Sporting side.

Xandao scored the only goal in the second half when he back-heeled in from close range following a free-kick.

City remain favourites to advance but they will have to be better in the return leg in Manchester on 15 March.

It could have been worse for Roberto Mancini's men, but, as he has done on a number of occasions this season, goalkeeper Joe Hart came to their rescue with a couple of superb saves, most notably from Ricky van Wolfswinkel's close-range shot during a period of pressure from the buoyant hosts after the opening goal.

City must do better than this if they are to keep their Europa League dream alive. Sporting were good value for their win. (*Sun*)

The home side take the lead through a sensational finish from centre-half **Xandao**. Matias Fernandez fires in a free-kick which Joe Hart can only parry out, Xandao's first effort is well saved by Hart but the defender has the presence of mind to improvise and flick in a marvellous back-heel into the net.

Sporting scored in the 51st minute and, although City rallied to dominate the closing 20 minutes, the home team could have scored one or two more in a second period that was certainly an improvement on a first half that threatened to send 35,000 people to sleep. (***Daily Mail***)

City were flat for large parts of the match and not only went home beaten but with concerns over the fitness of Vincent Kompany. (***Metro***)

Before the game Edin Dzeko angered Sporting by saying he had not heard of any of their players and it was left to Roberto Mancini to deny his side had shown any lack of respect to Sporting after slipping to a surprise defeat. (*Daily Express*)

Brazilian defender Xandao condemned a below-par Manchester City to defeat in the first leg of their Europa League tie against Sporting.

Xandao beat Joe Hart with a clever close-range back heel after 51 minutes as the Portuguese side controlled most of the last-16 encounter at the Jose Alvalade Stadium.

Hart also made two good saves, but City did have chances with Gareth Barry and Aleksandar Kolarov going close and Sergio Aguero almost breaking through late on.

Sporting's wastefulness, particularly early on, will give the Premier League leaders hope they can still turn the tie around at the Etihad Stadium. (*Sporting Life*)

City left in arrears by a lost night in Lisbon

Brazilian defender Xandao condemned City to defeat in the first leg of their Europa League last-16 tie in the Portuguese capital. City were flat for large parts of the match and not only went home beaten but with concerns over the fitness of Captain Vincent Kompany.

The game was only eight minutes old when Kompany began limping and he soon hobbled off with an injury which will concern City. The hosts started brightly in front of a vociferous crowd and Joe Hart was forced to make a decent save from a Joao Pereira shot, with Stijn Schaars dragging the rebound wide.

Sporting again looked bright following the break and the deadlock was broken after 51 minutes when Hart could only parry a Matias Fernandez free kick and despite saving superbly from Xandao, could do little to stop the defenders second attempt, a clever back heel.

Mario Balotelli replaced Edin Dzeko in the closing stages and the Italian crossed low into the home penalty area only to see David Silva shoot narrowly wide. City's attempts to secure an equaliser grew more frantic as time ran out but Sporting held firm.

MANAGEMENT VIEW

We try to play football but can lose sometimes, although I don't think we deserved to lose. I'm not surprised we lost because in football anything can happen.

We did not play very well and we could have scored, but we conceded a goal, so that is it.

We have another 90 minutes and it will be a different game. We still have a big chance. Hopefully we will have a chance to score and I think we will score. (**Roberto Mancini**)

SUPPORTERS' VIEWS

'Poor Performance from the lads and I have to say a strange team selection. We lacked the cutting edge but we will take them at home, no problems.'

'Very forgettable against a very average team.'

'Poor performance but I'm confident we will get through.'

'Worst performance of the season, back to our best next Thursday and we can easily beat this average side.'

'Sporting got a real cup atmosphere to help them in their biggest match of the season.'

'We underestimated Sporting. It didn't help Vincent going off, so early.'

'Probably City's worst performance of the season. Passing inaccurate and too slow. We can do much better than this.'

MANCHESTER CITY 3   SPORTING LISBON (SCP) 2

Goal Scorers: Aguero (2), Balotelli (P)
Europa League Cup
Round of 16 – Second Leg, Thursday 15 March 2012
City of Manchester Stadium
Attendance: 38,021

> **City Team:** Hart, Richards, Savic, K. Toure, Kolarov, Pizarro (Dzeko), Y. Toure, A. Johnson (De Jong), Silva (Nasri), Aguero, Balotelli
> Subs: Pantillimon (GK), Milner, Clichy, Roman

PRESS VIEW

Manchester City's fight back failed to save them from a shock Europa League exit on away goals to Sporting Lisbon.

Trailing 1-0 from the first leg in the last-16 tie, City fell further behind from a Matias Fernandez free-kick.

Ricky van Wolfswinkel made it 3-0 on aggregate before Sergio Aguero reduced the deficit, and Mario Balotelli's penalty made it 2-2 on the night.

Aguero scored again and goalkeeper Joe Hart was denied a spectacular winner when his header was saved at the death.

It was a dramatic finale as Hart, who had stayed in the box after going up for a corner, fired a powerful header towards the corner of the goal which Rui Patricio, his opposite number, saved brilliantly. **(BBC)**

Joe Hart almost scored what would have been a remarkable deciding goal, but there was to be no fairy tale ending. If you have to go out of Europe, this is how to do it, all guns blazing, all banners fluttering. (*Manchester Evening News*)

Late surge proves too little, too late for City

Sergio Aguero sparked a dramatic City fight back but Roberto Mancini's side paid for a dreadful first half display as they crashed out of the Europa League at the last-16 stage.

City looked down and out after a stunning Matias Fernandez free kick and a close Ricky Van Wolfswinkel strike which had Sporting up after 40 minutes, with City needing four goals to go through.

However the home side pulled one back on the hour through a fierce Aguero shot and when the Argentine was adjudged to have been tripped by Renato Neto, Balotelli nonchalantly dispatched the spot kick. With eight minutes left, Aguero hooked in from a corner to set up a nail-biting finale and in a last ditch effort, goalkeeper Joe Hart had a header brilliantly saved by his opposite number Rui Patricio.

MANAGEMENT VIEW

I am proud of the performance but disappointed for the two games. Today in the first half we didn't play. When I lose a game, I think why? I think because I made a mistake. The manager is the person who prepares for the game and I must have made mistakes. **(Roberto Mancini)**

I am very proud to be the leader of this team and to have these players working for me. It is great for the image of Sporting to knock out a club like Manchester City, who are one of the best teams in the world. **(Sporting coach)**

SUPPORTER'S VIEW

'I'm proud of the fight back which shows we have character in the squad, so onwards and upwards.'

2012-13 CHAMPIONS LEAGUE

Manchester City secured their return to the Champions League as the 2011-12 Premier League title holders, but the newly crowned winners entered Europe's top tier competition with a potentially daunting group stage task.

City were drawn to meet José Mourinho's Real Madrid in Champions League Group D, as well as Dutch champions Ajax and the German champions Borussia Dortmund. It is a group that has been billed the group of champions and following a draw at home to Ajax on Matchday 4 of the competition, it would appear that European Glory will have to be reserved for another season.

But those tales will have to be told another time...

Matchday 1 - Tuesday 18 September 2012
Real Madrid 3 Manchester City 2
Dzeko, Kolarov
Attendance: 70,380

City Team: Hart, Maicon (Zabaleta 75), Kompany, Nastasic, Clichy, Garcia, Yaya Toure, Silva (Dzeko 63), Barry, Tevez, Nasri (Kolarov 36)
Subs Not Used: Pantilimon, Lescott, Rodwell, Aguero

Matchday 2 - Wednesday 3 October 2012
Manchester City 1 Borussia Dortmund 1
Balotelli(P)
Attendance: 43,607

City Team: Hart, Zablaleta, Kompany, Nastasic, Clichy (Balotelli 80), Yaya Toure, Garcia (Rodwell 33), Nasri (Kolarov 55), Silva, Aguero, Dzeko
Subs Not Used: Pantilimon, Lescott, Milner, Tevez

Matchday 3 - Wednesday 24 October 2012
Ajax 3 Manchester City 1
Nasri
Attendance: 45,743

City Team: Hart, Richards, Clichy, Lescott (Kolarov 63), Kompany, Barry (Tevez 71), Milner (Balotelli 77), Yaya Toure, Nasri, Aguero, Dzeko
Subs Not Used: Pantilimon, Nastasic, Evans, Sinclair

Matchday 4 - Tuesday 6 November 2012
Manchester City 2 Ajax 2
Y Toure, Aguero
Attendance: 40,222

City Team: Hart, Zabaleta, Clichy, Kompany, Nastasic, Garcia (Balotelli 46), Barry (Kolarov 85), Y Toure, Nasri, Tevez (Dzeko 66), Aguero
Subs Not Used: Pantilimon, Maicon, Meppen-Walters, Sinclair

Matchday 5 - Wednesday 21 November 2012
Manchester City *vs* Real Madrid

Matchday 6 - Tuesday 4 December 2012
Borussia Dortmund *vs* Manchester City